Heart to Heart with Mary

A Yearly Devotional

God bless you. Mary keep you!
Mary Kathleen Glavich, SND

Mary Kathleen Glavich, SND

Scripture quotations in this book are from the New Revised Standard Version copyright © 1989, Division of Christian Education of the National Council of Churches of Christ in the United States of America.

Interior design and typesetting by
Mary Kathleen Glavich, SND

Cover photo by Mary Patricia Pasek, SND

ISBN-13: 978546423751
ISBN-10: 1546423753

Printed in the United States of America

Dedication

To Heidi Hess Saxton,
who conceived the idea for
Heart to Heart with Mary
and gave it direction.

Introduction

Heart to Heart with Mary

The Blessed Virgin Mary is the topic most requested for the talks and retreats I give. No wonder! This first-century Jewish woman is the Mother of God and our mother as well. By cooperating with God's plan, she became the mother of Jesus and helped to save the human race. By showing herself our caring and loving mother time and again, she has won a place in our hearts. Consequently, Mary is the subject of more paintings, statues, poems, songs, and books than any other woman. In fact, she has appeared on the cover of *Time* magazine at least ten times!

After one Marian retreat, a participant approached me and shared the story of her encounter with Mary. The woman said she was standing at the grave of her little girl, grieving. Distinctly she heard a voice say, "I will take care of your daughter, and I will take care of you." There was no one around. The distraught mother believed that it was Mary who spoke those comforting words to her.

Few people have actually heard Mary speak. We can imagine, though, what she would say to us in light of her being the best disciple of Jesus and our heavenly mother. I've done just that in this book. For each day of the year, Mary speaks to you, encouraging you to look to her as a model of virtue and as a strong advocate. She addresses you as "my child" because no matter what age a son or daughter is, to a mother her offspring is always her child. Some of Mary's daily little chats flow from feast days, her titles, or Marian devotions. At times she alludes to her earthly life and also reflects her awareness of today's world. After Mary's words there is a suggestion for responding to her and continuing the conversation.

My History with Mary

My own relationship with Mary blossomed when I transferred to a Catholic school as a preteen. I drew pictures of Our Lady, making her as beautiful as I could. One day my eighth-grade class visited Notre Dame Academy, an all-girls high school, for a concert. I vividly recall seeing at the end of a long hall a statue of Mary facing me. A strange and strong feeling came over me that my life would be bound up with this building, which also happened to be the motherhouse of the Sisters of Notre Dame. Indeed my life was; for I attended Notre Dame Academy, where I became the prefect of the Sodality (a Marian organization). After graduating, I joined the Sisters of Notre Dame and attended Notre Dame College.

Mary is the patroness of my religious community, and all of us have her name or some form of it in our religious name, which is why I am Sister *Mary* Kathleen. Inside our rings "All for Jesus through Mary" is engraved in French. Our Constitutions state about our Blessed Mother: "In her total dedication to God in faith and love, she is the model for our daily surrender to the ever-new call of the Lord" (no. 12).

When we are willing to surrender in this way, Mary's powerful intercession can truly change the course of our lives. Two evenings before writing this introduction, I received a call from a friend. Sobbing, she asked me to pray for her son. After being hospitalized for several days, the young man had undergone a six-hour surgery. A suspected blood clot in his arm near his heart was threatening his life. Immediately after the call, I made a holy hour during which I prayed a rosary and pleaded, "Mary, you understand what it is like to watch a son suffer. Please help keep my friend's son alive." The next day my friend e-mailed, "The doctors could find no blood clot. I believe that holy hour spared my son's life." Mary had come through once again. I'm sure she will hear your prayers as well.

The Purpose of *Heart to Heart with Mary*

Ten years ago I wrote *The Catholic Companion to Mary,* which helped me to know Mary more personally. This present book allowed me to strengthen my bond with her. Likewise, it enables my readers to cultivate a stronger relationship with Mary by hearing her speak to them as their own spiritual mother.

I believe this intimate conversation is vitally important for the spiritual life. While I was working on my previous book, a workman asked what I was writing. When I told him, he exclaimed, "Mary? I never pray to her. She's way up there like a goddess. What does she care about the dregs of my life?" I told him the story of Our Lady of Guadalupe. When she appeared to Saint Juan Diego in Mexico, she called him Juan Dieguito (an endearing form of his name) and "my dearest son." One day Juan Diego avoided meeting Mary at the appointed time because he was anxious to get a priest for his dying uncle. Mary appeared to him on the road anyway and chided, "Why are you worried? Am I not here, I who am your mother?" The uncle lived. Listening to this account, the workman was visibly moved and came to know Mary as his mother too.

Readers who already love Mary will delight in using *Chats with Mother Mary* to converse with her. People who ignore Mary, are ignorant of her, or are skeptical of devotion to her might be persuaded to look to her as their mother and model. It is my hope that my writing will not only inform people about our heavenly Mother, but spark a deeper devotion to her. Focusing on Mary, God's masterpiece, detracts nothing from Jesus. Rather, he is pleased when we love and honor his mother.

How to Use *Heart to Heart with Mary*
Sit in a quiet place and at a time when you will not be distracted by other people or the business of the day. You might set a chair facing you and imagine that Mary is seated there looking at you. Light a candle if you wish. Ask the Holy Spirit to open your heart to messages you need to hear.

Slowly read Mary's words and reflect on them. Then respond as suggested or in any way you are moved to converse with Mary. You might record your words in a journal.

Although this book offers a reflection for each day of the year and notes Mary's feast days, you can use the reflections as you wish:

• Make your way through the pages consecutively.

• Dip into the book at random.

• Feel free to skip around in the book and find a title that attracts you.

• On some days you might use more than one reflection during your time of prayer.

Retreats

Besides incorporating the conversations with Mary in your personal prayer routine, you may choose to use them as part of a private mini-retreat. Another option is to build a group retreat around them.*

My hope is that *Heart to Heart with Mary* will help fulfill for you the prayer that was often on St. Teresa of Kolkata's lips: "Mother of Jesus, be mother to me."

~ Mary Kathleen Glavich, SND

* In the back of this book is a resource for planning a shared retreat with a Marian theme.

January

Divine Motherhood
Solemnity of Mary, Mother of God

January 1

My child, it gives me great joy that you are carving out time in your busy day to talk with me. I'm eager for you to know me more personally. By becoming the Mother of God, I became your spiritual mother. I regard both roles as privileges. Yes, I'm in heaven with my son Jesus, but I'm also truly with you and ready to do everything in my power to see that you join us someday.

I hope that through our time together, you will realize the depth of my love for you. I want to help you to be happy and successful. When you are hurting, I want to comfort you. When you are confused, I want to counsel you. When you are besieged by temptations, I want to protect you. When you are in need, I want to plead to God for you. You will not be disappointed if you turn to me quickly and confidently, as a child does to its mother!

My supreme wish for you is that you possess the same wholehearted love of God that compelled me to give birth to Jesus. Then you too will bring him into the world.

cx *Tell Mary in which way you wish her to be a mother to you.*

Coping with Change

January 2

My child, in the course of your lifetime, you are bound to experience major shifts. The ground beneath your feet is always changing. Whether you are moving into a new neighborhood, switching jobs, or welcoming a child—whenever transition occurs, you may feel anxious or scared. But don't be afraid. God is always near you. That much never changes. I, too, am near you. That will never change either. I see you and know how you feel.

My life changed overnight when I was a sheltered girl living with my parents. One day I was playing with my friends, not worrying about anything more serious than if the bread would rise. Suddenly I was responsible for a husband and a baby, God's Son no less. Then we were fleeing to a foreign land to save my baby's life.

When you undergo or anticipate a change in your life, there is no need to panic. Trust in our loving Father's plan for you. Know that I walk right beside you every step of the way to calm your heart and strengthen you so you don't stumble or fall. We will face your uncertain future together, dear. Just keep a firm grasp on my hand. I won't let go.

ॐ *Does a change on the horizon frighten you? Talk to Mary about it.*

Time for Prayer

January 3

My child, sometimes your days are so crammed with activities that you wonder how you will ever get everything done. You scarcely have time to eat, much less pray, and you feel bad about that. When you are in this bind, don't worry or grow frustrated. I am aware of your desire to keep in touch with me through prayer, and I love you for it. When you are prevented from praying, I miss you, but I understand. So does your heavenly Father.

As you carry out your countless responsibilities, you can always send me short "arrow prayers." I often prayed like this. For instance, when I looked up briefly from mending a tunic and saw my boy Jesus outside wrestling with a friend, I would pray, "Thank you, God, for this miracle."

Speak to me briefly throughout your day, my dear child. Say beautiful words like, "Mary, I love you" and "My Mother, my hope." I would love it if you made these occasional aspirations a habit. That way we would stay close. I would know that you are thinking about me. Believe me, you are always on my mind and in my heart.

   ❧ *Today practice "arrow prayers" as you move through the day. Write about the experience this evening. Did it make you feel closer to Mary?*

Star of Evangelization

January 4

My child, on the day you were baptized, you received a mission to evangelize. As a follower of my son, you are responsible for bringing other people to him. Jesus told his apostles to be fishers of people, even to go out into the deep water.[1] He depends on you to catch men and women for him, too. You might find this task intimidating. It may make you uncomfortable. I understand that it is not easy nowadays to talk about Jesus, to explain your faith, and to invite people to follow him with you. People tend to avoid speaking about religion because it embarrasses them or because they do not wish to offend others.

Long ago I was an evangelizer, actually the first one to reveal Jesus. I showed him to shepherds, magi, Simeon and Anna in the Temple, waiters at the wedding in Cana, not to mention our neighbors in Nazareth. Ask me and I will entreat the Holy Spirit to embolden you to speak about Jesus. Keep in mind that loving deeds may be more effective than words in luring people to Jesus. Either way, I'll be glad to lend a hand in filling your net and bringing people safely to shore. You can rely on me, your mother, to be a good partner.

ɔ *What strategies can you adopt to announce the Good News to others? Talk them over with Mary.*

---

[1] Luke 5:4

Confiding Crosses

January 5

My child, difficulties — like weeds in a garden —
crop up in everyone's life. You might suppose that as the
Mother of God I would have enjoyed a charmed life. Quite
the opposite was true. My yes to God came at a cost. As
Jesus' mother, I endured scandal and hardship, fear and
grief. Don't ever suppose that your adversities and pain
are God's punishment for something you did. You may
have brought them on yourself. Otherwise, they may be a
means to purify you as gold is purified and strengthened
by fire.

Complaining about a cross doesn't make it lighter.
Instead it casts a shadow over the day for you and for
your listeners. Dwelling on your trouble, only magnifies
the burden. "Come to me," my son invites. He knows how
unbearably heavy a cross can be.

Just as I stood with Jesus in his passion, I stand
with you as you bear the weight of your crosses. When
you need to talk, never hesitate to share your trials with
me! Don't wait until you reach the breaking point. I
always have a listening ear and a shoulder to cry on for
you. I'm right here. Feel free to pour out your heart to me,
dear. Let me soothe you and help you endure.

℘ *Does something weigh you down? Talk to Mary about it.*

God's Little Graces
Epiphany

January 6

My child, every once in a while, our good God steps into lives in unexpected ways. How amazed I was when the magi carrying precious gifts appeared at our house. Their visit reassured me that my son was indeed the Messiah.

Sometimes God "winks" at you. That is, he arranges epiphanies to remind you of his presence guiding your life. Of course, your heavenly Father is not the only one who likes to surprise you. As your mother, I do, too, and work behind the scenes to send little serendipities to punctuate your life.

Maybe when you were searching for a fact, a book opened to the right page. Or maybe on a plane you were seated next to someone who gave you needed advice. You might not even ask me for small favors like these, but I love bestowing them on you, for I am your mother who loves you more than you can imagine. Remember these supernatural courtesies as special moments in our relationship. Don't dismiss them or conclude that you were only dreaming. Cherish them as acts of love.

Talk to Mary about unexpected graces that have come to you. Write them down as they occur to encourage you during difficult times and to remind you of God's love.

Welcome Interruptions

January 7

My child, interruptions can be frustrating. You might have your whole day planned out, but then a friend drops by unexpectedly or a ferocious storm arises or a blinding headache comes on suddenly. But consider this dear: while you may be stewing, God's timing is perfect. Believe me.

I know from experience that this is how our heavenly Father tends to work. An angel interrupted my marriage plans, Herod interrupted our plans to return to Nazareth, and once Jesus interrupted our plans to return home after the Passover. Each time I had a choice: to resist and rail against God or to trust him, knowing that he is all-wise and pure love.

When you meet up with a detour in your day, learn to accommodate. Don't waste your energy balking at the inevitable. When you gracefully accept interruptions, I smile at your humility and maturity, my beloved child. And remember . . . inconveniences can often turn out to be blessings in disguise!

ဢ *Can you recall a recent interruption that turned out to be a blessing? Share that memory with Mary.*

In Need of Help
Our Lady of Prompt Succor

January 8

My child, during the times you walk a perilous path, I'm concerned about you. You may encounter grave danger from natural disasters: fire, floods, tornadoes, hurricanes, or earthquakes. Enemies may conspire against you. Problems regarding your family, your job, your health, or your finances might seem insurmountable. What threatens you may be minor, but nonetheless upsetting and robbing you of sleep. No matter what disturbs your peace, at the first sign of it, you can look to me with confidence for help. As quickly as any mother speeds to her child in distress, I will hurry to your aid. I will protect and defend you. I promise.

So let me wrap you in the protecting folds of my mantle and clasp you close to my heart until what frightens you passes by and your fear dissipates. Through me, God rescued all people. And through me, your compassionate mother, love and mercy flow to you when you are in distress. You can look forward to my unending help until the end of your days on earth.

ଔ *Let Mary know about anything troubling you today. Tell her you have confidence in her and her love for you.*

Accepting Yourself

January 9

My child, because you are human, there are probably days when you are not happy with yourself. Perhaps you made a silly mistake or an appointment slipped your mind. Maybe you spoke carelessly and hurt a friend's feelings. When things like this happen, you might be tempted to be hard on yourself. But let me reassure you: you are a treasure!

I may not have been the smartest girl in the village or the most talented, but I had my own gifts. So do you. God made you a unique, irreplaceable individual. You were created out of love in God's image and likeness. You have dignity as God's beloved child and mine as well as an incredible destiny. True, you give God glory by using your gifts—but you also honor and please him by gracefully accepting your flaws and weaknesses in all humility.

When your self-confidence is waning, come quickly to me. I will tenderly embrace you and whisper in your ear how wonderful you really are and how much I love you. Then, if necessary, I will help you to mend what has been broken or to start again.

ℂℳ *Are there things you don't like about yourself? Speak to Mary about them.*

Little Things

January 10

My child, sometimes little things make all the difference. It warmed my heart when I caught Joseph looking at me with love, when a woman passing by on the street told me I had lovely eyes, and when Jesus held me close the day Joseph died. You probably won't accomplish great things and become famous. You might not appear on television or write a bestseller. You might not even achieve your life's dreams. These things don't really matter. I certainly don't care if you're not a huge success in the eyes of the world.

What I wish for you is to be holy, and holiness for the most part consists in doing little things with great love. That is what sweetens life for everyone. I witness your hidden acts of love and your faithfulness in little things, my darling, and as your mother I'm proud of you for them. They will not earn you a place in the hall of fame on earth, but know that your name will be inscribed in the Book of Life. It is also written on my heart.

℞ *What little kind things have people done for you? Tell Mary about them and how they made you feel.*

Your Model

January 11

My child, you could say about me and Jesus, "like mother, like son." Not only do we share the same physical features, but our two immaculate hearts are perfectly in tune. We possess the same virtues to perfection. We also burn with the same love for God and for people. I am your mother, too, in the spiritual realm. How I wish you were a spitting image of me! Then you would also be full of grace and pleasing to God.

Holiness is not an impossible quest for you. It's within your reach because the Holy Spirit, the Sanctifier, dwells in your heart. Besides, I will be happy to obtain certain graces for you. All you have to do is ask me.

Read what Scripture and the Church say about me. Ponder my qualities — my faithfulness, obedience, selflessness, humility, gentleness, kindness, and purity. Then try to reflect them. I will help you. The more you resemble me, the more you will be like Jesus. And isn't that the main goal of a Christian — to be Jesus in the world today, to be another incarnation?

☙ *Choose one of Mary's characteristics you would like to imitate. Talk to her about how you can reflect it.*

A Courageous Heart

January 12

My child, are you afraid you'll be laughed at for living your faith? Do you find it difficult to keep God's laws? Are the responsibilities of your vocation onerous? As your loving mother, I encourage you to be brave. Carry out God's will for you with courage and confidence.

At your baptism, the same Holy Spirit who empowered me flooded your soul with abundant gifts, including the virtue of fortitude. As you encounter adversities and setbacks, soldier on. You are stronger than you think.

I am with you, surrounding you with my love like a protective cloak. When I lived on earth, I was a strong, valiant woman, tanned from the Galilee sun and toned from manual labor. I did not shy away from the difficult moments of my life as mother of the Savior. Remember, I faced criticism and hardship and loneliness. Draw on me for inspiration as you climb the steep, rugged mountains along the path of your life's journey. Lean on me for strength. You will find me an unfailing help.

Talk to Mary about a problem you must tackle and ask her assistance.

Our Lady, Undoer of Knots

January 13

My child, as a young woman, frequently I had to untangle knots and snarls in the strands of wool and linen I wove making clothing for my family. It could be so aggravating! Everyone experiences these trying moments: in shoelaces, cords, yarn, and strings of Christmas lights. Each time you encounter such knots, let them remind you that I am here to help you undo those intangible knots and tangles that complicate your life.

Sometimes I sit and watch proudly as you summon the patience to straighten these knots out for yourself. On other days my heart aches for you as you struggle unsuccessfully to solve your problems. Sometimes you only make them worse!

My child, when you come to me with your predicaments and lay them in my lap, I will help you untangle and smooth them. All my attention will be focused on giving you relief. So do remember to entrust your problems to me! Let me assist you in perplexing situations, both large and small. I want you to experience a life full of joy! After all, that is what loving mothers desire for their children.

ᘓ *What knots are currently hampering your life? Put them in Mary's hands.*

The Value of Friendship

January 14

My child, what a blessing friends are! They accept you for who you are and give good advice. You laugh and cry together. Friends help you out. More than once when I needed flour or olives, a neighbor came to my aid. A high point in my day was going to the well each morning where we women would talk about our children and husbands and swap tips about the market. I will always remember how my friends supported me on the worst day of my life—the day my son was killed. They stood around me at the foot of the cross and cried with me.

I thank God with you for the good friends, young and old, who brighten your days. I smile when I see you together enjoying one another's company. I would like it if you realized that I am your friend, too. In fact, I'm one of your best friends. I only want what is good for you. By the way, I'm not a fair-weather friend, but I stand by you in thick and thin. You can count on me. I'll never let you down, dear.

ଔ *Talk to Mary about your friends past and present. Ask her to keep them in her loving care.*

Praying Psalms

January 15

My child, I love the psalms — and not only because many of these prayer-songs were composed by my ancestor King David! No matter what mood I was in, there was always a psalm to express it. After Jesus died, I realized that Psalm 22 described his suffering in detail. I treasured the psalms as a gift from God.

As your mother who desires that you grow spiritually, I have some advice. At every Mass you pray a responsorial psalm with the community. Pray psalms on your own at home, too. When you are in trouble, pray a lament psalm like Psalm 13 that begins, "How long, O Lord?" When your heart swells with joy at the goodness of God, pray a psalm of praise like Psalm 150. Do some psalms puzzle you? I will ask the Holy Spirit to enlighten your mind to understand them.

You might learn a few psalms by heart, at least certain verses. As you pray a psalm, think of me at your side praying with you. Our voices will combine in praise of God, a foretaste of what we will be doing together eternally in heaven. I can't wait!

℘ *Pray a psalm. Share with Mary what it means to you.*

The Power of Words

January 16

My child, words have power to bring about earthshaking events. Consider what happened after I said, yes to God and after Jesus commanded, "Lazarus, come forth." Think what occurs when a priest states, "This is my body." Pope Francis suggested three phrases for a happy marriage: "May I?" "Thank you," and "Pardon me."

People's words can lift you to cloud nine or they can plunge you into a dark pit. I rejoice when someone praises or compliments you. And when someone speaks harshly or cruelly to you, I cringe and feel your pain.

You have uttered things that you regret. You may have been hurt, angry, or just thoughtless. Don't flog yourself over it. The Bible says, "Anyone who makes no mistakes in speaking is perfect."[2] We both know you are not perfect!

I brought forth into the world the Word made flesh and taught him to speak. When you find it hard to control your tongue, pray to me, my dear child. My words were always gentle and life-giving. I will gladly teach you to speak kindly and lovingly.

ೞ *Recall words that filled you with joy and words that cut you to the heart. Talk to Mary about them.*

---

[2] James 3:2

Rest and Relaxation

January 17

My child, when you are stressed by work, I worry about you and wish you wouldn't take on so much. Be careful that you are not so overwhelmed with things to do at home and at work that you don't take time to rest and have fun once in a while. For good reason Scripture says that after the work of creation, our good God spent a whole day resting. At our house in Nazareth, we observed the Sabbath. Joseph closed the shop, and we spent Saturday enjoying one another's company, visiting with friends and relatives, and praying.

You needn't feel guilty when you occasionally go on a vacation, read, or play games. I'm relieved when you do such things that are good for your health and sanity. Remember that the commandment "Thou shalt not kill" implies that you take care of yourself, my dear!

One way I propose that you rest is to take a little break occasionally and spend time with me. Focus on my loving presence and let the cares of the day's business vanish from your mind. I will help you finish your projects and chores in ways that may surprise you.

ଓ *Tell Mary what you like to do in free time. Plan with her how to provide adequate rest for yourself.*

Oneness

January 18

My child, today I come with a favor to ask of you. At the Last Supper, my son prayed that all may be one. That is also my prayer. Jesus is distressed because his followers are splintered into many separate groups. Sometimes these groups compete, bicker over theology, and, yes, even fight. This doesn't entice anyone to follow Jesus! Because he is distressed by this, I am too. How I wish all of my children would get along! I would spread my mantle wide and encompass all of them, drawing them near to me and to one another.

What can you do to fulfill my wish? Speak to people in other faith traditions. Learn what they believe and what you have in common with them. You may find this a challenging task, but with my help you will have the determination and the wisdom to carry it out.

Above all, pray to me that divisions may be mended. I have the ear of our heavenly Father, and I will ask him to bless your efforts for unity. By striving to fulfill my important request, you will have my eternal gratitude and my son's.

ᛒ *Ask Mary to help you see how you can promote unity.*

Tender Love

January 19

My child, I am your heavenly mother whose heart overflows with love for you. From the day you drew your first breath and let out your first cry, I have been watching over you. St. Catherine Labouré regarded me as her mother. When I appeared to her, she sped to where I sat, knelt, and rested her hands on my lap. I was moved by this familiar gesture.

I know what you are thinking now: "I can't see you. I can't rest my hands in your lap and look into your eyes." But trust me, although your senses don't perceive me, I am real and alive. I am with you, dear, just in another dimension. Here I am, looking at you and loving you with all the tender sweetness of a mother's love. I care deeply about you. I'm interested in what you will do and say and feel today. I want to protect you from life's hurts and from anything that might imperil your eternal salvation. I want to be your helper as you travel through violent storms and across arid deserts on your way home, where you will finally behold me. Nothing you do can ever destroy the bond between us.

ଓ *Talk to Mary about how she is a mother to you.*

The Trinity

January 20

My child, the entire Trinity dwells in the depths of your being. Do you tend to direct your prayers to one Person in particular and somewhat ignore the other two? I am intimately related with each Person of the Trinity. I am daughter of the Father, Mother of the Son, and spouse of the Holy Spirit. You, too, enjoy a special relationship with each Person. Therefore, I encourage you to nurture all three relationships.

The Father is your creator, who made you to share divine life. Praise him. The Son is your redeemer, who atoned for your sins. Thank him. And the Holy Spirit is your sanctifier. Ask him for the grace to become the holy person you are meant to be. All three Persons love you with infinite, unimaginable love. And because I love you, I hope that your love for each holy Person grows more intense as you come to know them better.

Whenever you make the Sign of the Cross or pray the Glory Be, you proclaim the mystery of our Triune God. Be conscious of the words. Imagine how slowly and reverently I pronounce them. Then do likewise.

℞ *Ask Mary to help you know, love, and honor each Person of the Trinity.*

Unfailing Loyalty

January 21

My child, loyalty is a prized quality that I'm sure you admire and would like to possess. Ruth, who was King David's ancestor and ours too, is esteemed for her loyalty to her mother-in-law Naomi. Ruth left her home, relatives, and native land and gave up her religion to befriend Naomi. Ruth refused to forsake her. If only Judas, Peter, and other apostles had been that loyal to Jesus before he died! Would you please be loyal to my son? Defend him when necessary, speak up for him, and do as he asks. He will reward you for your loyalty someday, good king that he is.

Be assured that I will always be loyal to you. I, your heavenly mother, will walk at your side, intercede to God for you, and guide you all the days of your life. Even if you turn away from God or if you ignore me, I will still be with you. When you are upset, I will soothe you with a gentle touch. When you are in trouble, I won't forsake you. I didn't abandon my son when he was tortured and killed. No one on earth would ever be as faithful to you, my dear, as I am.

℣ *On whose loyalty do you depend? Talk to Mary about them and ask her to pray for them.*

Generous Praise

January 22

My child, when someone compliments you, lovely warm feelings of joy and satisfaction wash over you. This is also true for other people, so be lavish with praise. At times you might think well of others for something—a character trait, an achievement, or their appearance—but it doesn't occur to you to express this to them. Praising is an act of love, a gift. People like to know that their good qualities or work is recognized. Ask me to prompt you to voice your thoughts when an occasion arises for you to praise someone. I'll be happy to do so.

I'm aware of your wonderful qualities and the many good things you do even secretly. Interiorly hear my voice praising you. Know that I am proud of you for countless reasons, my child. On the other hand, it pleases me to hear you praise me in prayers like the Hail Mary and in hymns. This is not because I crave compliments for myself but because anything praiseworthy about me is due to the gracious One who created me. Your praise of me redounds to the glory of God.

ଔ *Tell Mary the qualities you admire in her. Ask her to pray that you imitate them. Sing a hymn in praise of her.*

A Holy Couple
Espousals of Our Lady

January 23

My child, in God's great design, my vocation was to be a married woman and a mother. How relieved I was when Joseph married me after I was pregnant. Having a husband protected me not only from scorn but death, the penalty for unwed mothers. Joseph was a good man and deeply loved Jesus and me. I couldn't have asked for a better partner in life. Ours was truly a marriage made in heaven!

God also personally planned your vocation as the best route for you to get to heaven. Trust God to provide the graces to see you through all the ups and downs this path entails. Have no regrets about the lifestyle to which your heart has drawn you.

As the mother of Jesus, I am also your loving mother. God has entrusted you to me to ensure that you stay close to him. As you carry out the responsibilities of your state in life, look to me for support and guidance. Being your heavenly mother is not a chore for me but a pleasure. I feel blessed to have you as my child.

ଔ *What challenges are you finding as you live your vocation?*
   Confide them to Mary and ask her help.

Meeting Jesus

January 24

My child, you are one of a long line of people who believe in Jesus and follow his teachings. I was the first Christian: the first person to hear the Good News and one of the first to look into the face of Jesus. You can imagine the conversations Jesus and I had over meals during the thirty years we lived together! I wish you could know my son as well as I do. What profound peace and joy you would have. Nothing would disturb you.

You meet my Jesus when you read about him in the Gospels and ponder what he did and said. You also come to know Jesus better when you learn what others say about him. But most of all, as your loving mother, I urge you to speak with him. He dwells within you, longing for your attention. He looks on you with love in his eyes the way I look on you, my child. Share the happenings of the day with Jesus. Tell him your hopes and fears. Then listen to what he says in your heart. Your love for my son will grow as mine did. My motherly dream for you is that you will live with me and Jesus forever, enjoying eternal bliss.

ଔ *How would you describe your relationship with Jesus? Ask Mary to pray that you may strengthen it every day.*

God's Reed

January 25

My child, I've been compared to a reed, an instrument through which God played his song of love. This analogy is apt because through me God showed the depth of his love for human beings. You too are called to be a reed through which God plays a love song to people. Place yourself in God's hands, dear, and let him use you to reveal his love to the world. I will be only too glad to assist you in being gentle, kind, humble, loving, and forgiving. Then seeing and hearing you, people will be drawn to God as though entranced by a beautiful, mystical melody. Goodness attracts.

I know that on some days depression, ennui, or discouragement overwhelm you. When that happens, you feel like a broken reed, only capable of producing sour notes. You don't think you can help yourself, much less other people. Don't despair. To me, you still have great possibilities. You have only to turn to me with confidence, my child. I can obtain the grace to mend and strengthen you. You will be as good as new, a fitting instrument for God, like I was.

ભ *Talk to Mary about your desire to be a channel of God's love.*

Leave Mistakes Behind

January 26

My child, do you ever doubt yourself because of past failures? Regret decisions you made, especially those that hurt others or complicated your life? Wish you could take back words you said? You are not alone. Sometimes I thought things such as, Maybe I shouldn't have gone with Joseph to Bethlehem when I was nine months pregnant. You make choices according to the light you are given at the time. Perhaps at times you do not foresee unwelcome consequences that could stem from them.

Don't worry about errors you made in the past. What is done is done. Keep in mind that our God is good and draws good out of any situation, including your all-too-human mistakes.

Do you think that I judge you harshly for your failings or think any less of you? Of course not! Rather, I sympathize with you, my beloved child. The last thing I want is for regret to gnaw away at you, eroding your happiness. Come, bury your mistakes in my heart and forget them. Then walking together, let's face the future with confidence and hope.

ભ *Entreat Mary to help you to forget your failings and to move on with your life.*

Expect a Miracle

January 27

My child, you might need something major, such as a cure, the sale of your house, or a good spouse. You pray, thinking you are asking for a miracle. Never fear. The Angel Gabriel assured me that nothing is impossible for God. Jesus claimed that if you have faith, you can move mountains.[3] Count on your heavenly Father, who has the utmost love for you, to answer your prayer. He might reply, "No," but only when what you ask isn't for the best. However, God may respond, "All in good time. Just be patient" or "No, I have a better idea." And God might answer your prayer in an astounding manner.

I witnessed miracles—a virgin birth, water becoming wine, and the dead raised to life. God who caused these amazing things has power to work miracles for you, too, even in small matters. In fact, he delights in making you happy. So look to God with hope and don't give up pleading for your need. And remember to enlist my help, my beloved child. I'm always ready to add my prayers to yours. God doesn't say no to his mother.

ᦉ *Is there a special need pressing on your heart? Speak to Mary about it.*

---

[3] Matthew 17:20

Mary's Gratitude

January 28

My child, you may be surprised, but today I wish to tell you that my heart is bursting with gratitude to you. Yes! Thank you for your tireless efforts to follow my son. I know at times it isn't easy to be a Christian. Thank you for your prayers and sacrifices for my suffering children — the sick, the needy, those in war torn countries, sinners, and the poor souls. Thank you for the numerous acts of love you perform for people you know as well as for strangers. And thank you for spreading the Gospel to others by your words and deeds.

In a special way, thank you for the tokens of love you offer me — your prayers to me like the Rosary and your devotions like setting flowers before my image and going to an extra Mass on Saturday, my day. These things mean a great deal to me because I love you so very much, my darling.

Jesus, too, appreciates all of these acts I've mentioned. I look forward to the day when he and I will be able to thank you face-to-face.

☙ *You have many reasons to be grateful to Mary. Enumerate them for her and thank her.*

Nuisances

January 29

My child, every life is peppered with nuisances. To me, hot weather and insects in our house were annoying. So was having to grind grain every day. You may be bothered by noisy neighbors, an allergy, or a piece of equipment that doesn't work right. How do you react to irritating things? You can let them get to you, lose sleep over them, and cultivate an ulcer. You might become irritable yourself and upset others!

Because I care about you, dear, I recommend a much wiser course, that is, to take steps to dispel the problems. If that doesn't work, a change in attitude might. My son was exasperated at times by thickheaded disciples and critical religious leaders. Jesus accepted his frustration as part of the sacrifice of becoming human. When you aren't able to remedy a situation, why not transform it by offering it up? Then it will be put to good use. Or here is another idea: Instead of concentrating on your nuisances, set your mind on me. This will restore calm and peace to your troubled heart.

ଔ *What are your pet peeves? Speak to Mary about them and ask her help in dealing with them.*

Bridge to Jesus

January 30

My child, an expression dear to Christians and to me is "To Jesus through Mary." I take you to my son. Don't ever think that devotion to me is not important, an option on the periphery of your faith. No, it is a vital key to a thriving spiritual life. Praying to me doesn't detract at all from Jesus. In his love for you, he gave me to you as a mother, someone who cherishes and protects you. He is pleased when you take advantage of his gift by treating me as your heavenly mother.

I brought Jesus into the world so that he could mingle with men and women. Today I serve as a bridge leading people like you to him. Faithfully I make known your needs to my son. I pass on to him your pleas for help and speak up for you. When you reflect on and imitate my virtues, you are actually conforming yourself to the heart of Jesus. My son has arranged that graces empowering you to live as he taught pass through my compassionate hands. The more you love and honor me, the more Jesus will bless you. I promise you.

ℛ *Do you know people who don't realize the benefits of having Mary as a mother? Ask Mary to enlighten them, perhaps through you.*

Modest Goals

January 31

My child, I shook my head when I heard that Salome's two sons argued over who would have the higher place in heaven. It's natural to desire fame, power, and esteem, but my son cautioned again that tendency. He taught that the last would be first. That was true for me. In Nazareth, I was "just Mary," the wife of the carpenter Joseph. But now I am exalted higher than the angels!

When you hunger for a high position, awards, notoriety, or praise, I'm afraid for you. It may mean that you consider yourself better than others. Aiming at being glorified is a sign of pride and ends in disaster. To keep dangerous ambitions in check, look to me. I will teach you to strive for what really matters: holiness. This is achieved through humility, meekness, and obedience—in other words, by resembling Jesus, who never lorded over others but ministered to their needs.

Whenever you have the urge to aspire to being raised above others, call upon me. I will ask God to set your heart on what pleases him. Even if few people know your name, you are precious in my eyes.

> ℘ *Examine your goals in Mary's presence. Ask her what she thinks of them.*

February

Guilt, Be Gone!

February 1

My child, do past sins and embarrassing, uncomfortable memories weigh like heavy stones on your heart? If so, this saddens me, for I want nothing more than for you to be completely happy. You are only human, prone to weaknesses and lapses. But you are also a beloved child of God and my own dear child. We love and understand you, no matter what.

If only you would see yourself as I see you: a reflection of God's image and likeness, and a person whose destiny is eternal glory. If only you would love yourself as I love you. I know you through and through, and realize that you desire to be good and to follow in the way of my son. Let the past failings stored in your mind melt away as you turn your heart toward God and receive his mercy.

I will gladly obtain many blessings for you from my divine son to help you obey God and live the Gospel values. Rise above your guilt and embrace grace.

℘ *What sin or fault do you find most difficult to overcome? Ask Mary for the grace to be free of it, once and for all.*

Obeying Laws
Purification of the Blessed Virgin Mary
February 2

My child, you prove your love for God by obeying him and lawful authorities. Joseph and I were good, faithful Jews who followed our religious laws. Forty days after Jesus was born, we took him to the Temple because our religion required that the firstborn be presented to God. On the same day, I fulfilled the law that women be purified after giving birth. You might reason that Jesus and I were exempt from these laws, and you would be right. Still, we obeyed them.

I would like you to love God so much that you do whatever he wishes. This means obeying the Ten Commandments he gave Moses and also following Church laws. I realize that it is hard to keep some of God's laws today when doing so makes you countercultural and perhaps mocked and shunned. You might not even agree with or understand them. I will be with you in your struggles to live rightly. I will firmly hold onto you as you make your way through the currents that threaten to sweep you off course. Trust in my everlasting love for you, my dear.

ை *What law is hard for you to observe? Talk to Mary about it and ask her to give you the strength and love to follow it.*

Living with Less
February 3

My child, wealth is not the most important thing in the world. It won't solve all your problems. When Joseph and I presented Jesus in the Temple, we sacrificed two turtledoves because we couldn't afford a lamb. We were not desperately poor, but we weren't well-to-do either. Our home was a simple two-room structure with few furnishings. Still we were happy.

Nowadays many people aren't satisfied until they own the latest gadget, the trendiest clothing, or the most expensive jewelry. They hope to get rich quick. In many cases, the wealthy learn that money and possessions do not guarantee happiness and can even destroy it.

I pray that you avoid the trap of accumulating more and more because I want only the best for you. Jesus taught that you should let your treasure be in heaven.[4] He is your greatest treasure, and you will possess him by sharing with those in need. Then you will experience the deep down joy I desire for you, my dear. In heaven there is no money at all, but we are all perfectly happy.

ౢ *Talk to Mary about ways you can share what you own.*

---

[4] Matthew 6:20

Gift of the Elderly

February 4

My child, old age is a gift for the elderly, and these people are a gift to you. At Jesus' Presentation we met Simeon and Anna, who were advanced in age. Both had been faithful all their lives and were rewarded by beholding Jesus, the Messiah for whom they had prayed so long. Meeting them was a grace for me. No doubt you know elderly people, perhaps your grandparents, neighbors, or parishioners. They may be infirm or forgetful. They might not know how to operate modern inventions. But they possess the wisdom of experience.

Cherish these older people and make them feel loved. Converse with them, consult them, and perform little services for them. That is what I would do. Those older children of mine are sometimes overlooked in society and lonely. They may be in great pain. God will bless you for your kindness to them, and my love for you will increase.

God willing, you may live for many years, too. Don't worry about your future for a minute. No matter how old you become, you will always be my child. I will take care of you until your last breath.

ଔ *Ask Mary to help you show love to the elderly in your life.*

Bittersweet Times

February 5

My child, sometimes an event causes great happiness as well as deep sorrow. The Presentation of Jesus comes to mind. What a joy it was to hear Simeon confirm that my baby would be the Messiah, a light to Gentiles and for glory to Israel. But then he foretold that Jesus would be opposed and a sword would pierce my soul. My heart sank.

You also live through experiences that evoke both joy and sadness. You don't know whether to laugh or cry. Maybe you receive a diploma, but your father is not there to celebrate with you. Or on your wedding day, you learn that a friend has cancer. On such bittersweet occasions, thank your heavenly Father for the good fortune he sent you. As for the bad fortune God allowed to happen, depend on me to walk with you through it with my arm lovingly around your shoulders. I will always be your companion in tough times, offering you comfort and strength. I will help you to focus on the rainbow, not the black storm clouds and remind you that an eternity of unalloyed joy awaits you at the end of the road.

cos *Talk to Mary about one of your bittersweet experiences.*

Entrusting Yourself to Mary

February 6

My child, to consecrate means to set something apart for God or for sacred use. Towns and cities have been consecrated to me. Popes have consecrated the whole world to me! What touches my heart most is when people entrust themselves to me by a personal act of consecration. I propose this to you today. In consecrating yourself to me, you offer me your whole life, your heart, and all you are and do. You place yourself under my special protection. Consecration is an excellent way to express your love and devotion to me, dear.

By making an act of consecration to me, ultimately you are consecrating yourself to Jesus and honoring God. It implies that you have your heart set on becoming holy.

If you would like to belong to me in a special way, pray an act of consecration. This will confirm that I am indeed your spiritual mother. It will also make you even more conscious of the crucial role I play in your life and my unfailing love for you. I would like that very much.

℞. *Pray: My Queen, my Mother! I give myself entirely to you, and to show my devotion to you I consecrate to you this day, my eyes, my ears, my mouth, my heart, my whole being without reserve. Wherefore, good Mother, as I am your own, keep me, guard me, as your property and possession.*

Servanthood

February 7

My child, service is the hallmark of a Christian. My son is a shining example of it. He served his Father and all of us by becoming human and surrendering his life. While on earth, Jesus ministered to thousands of needy people. He asked his followers to be servants like him and demonstrated by washing the apostles' feet.

You recall that when the Angel Gabriel proposed God's plan, I declared myself God's servant. I am still a servant today. I serve you as your mother who lovingly takes cares of you and acts as your ambassador in heaven.

A child of mine does not expect to be waited on. Take after Jesus and me and regard yourself as a servant. When someone needs help, spring into action. When an opportunity arises to volunteer, sign up. How pleased I am when I see you picking up the towel!

Are you afraid that you lack the heart, the skills, or the time to care for others? No problem. When you ask me for help, I will hurry to your side. I will see that you are equipped to carry out any task that involves serving. Then you will be a channel of love, a real Christian.

℘ *How do you serve others? How could you serve them? Ask Mary to open your eyes to ways.*

The Luxury of Silence

February 8

My child, your world is hectic and noisy compared to mine in Galilee. God's voice is sometimes drowned out! I feel sorry for you. Hear my son invite you, "Come away and rest a while." He took time out from the clamoring crowds that followed him. I wish you would too for your own wellbeing.

Find a quiet place where you can hear God's gentle whisper in your heart. Contemplate there the beauty of God's creation. Listen to the birds chirping, the waves crashing, or the leaves rustling. Ponder the life and words of Jesus and the mysteries of my life. Most of all, commune with God and with me. Our constant presence with you will become more obvious when you are not distracted by noise.

You need peaceful oases to bolster your spiritual life and your relationship with God and with me. You will find them both a calming relief and a sweet experience. Believe me, you will come away refreshed and ready to face whatever challenges your future holds. Those minutes spent in silence and prayer will be the most important and relished ones in your day.

ଓ *Talk to Mary about when and where you can enjoy silence.*

Want to Complain? Refrain!

February 9

My child, when things go wrong, you are liable to complain. It's only human. I felt like complaining plenty of times: when Joseph came late for supper, when the cheese got moldy, when rain prevented me from doing laundry, or when I was cheated at the market. As much as I was tempted to vent, I held my tongue.

Because I love you, I must point out that while complaining might make you feel better, it also might make you feel worse. Constant complaining drives people away from you. Besides, airing your troubles has ill effects on your hearers. It makes them feel bad for you and may remind them of their comparable problems. Complaining is contagious. The upshot is that good moods evaporate and spirits are dragged down. Keeping your little disappointments to yourself shows love for others.

When annoying things happen — when people let you down, when you have a headache, or when your plans don't work out — share them with me. I will be happy to listen and won't be harmed by it as others might be. In my loving arms you will find the comfort you seek.

ଔ *Share with Mary anything you have to complain about. Ask her to help you keep from complaining to others.*

Faced with Mystery

February 10

My child, you grapple with immense questions: why am I here, how did the universe start, is there really an afterlife, and why do the good suffer? I wrestled with the same questions. In addition, all through my life I dealt with unique personal mysteries. Why did God choose me? How could the baby nestled in my arms be God the Son? And most vexing to me, why did my son undergo such horrendous sufferings and a shameful death?

You won't have the satisfaction of learning the answers to the most mystifying questions here on earth. I realize that this is a hardship for you. I pray that as you explore the mysteries, you never doubt God or lose faith. You need to trust in God's love for you and believe that his divine providence is working everything out for the good. From my perspective in heaven, I can assure you, dear child, that this is absolutely true.

Take heart. At the end of time, many things will be revealed to you. For the present, what I hope is very clear to you is my loving companionship while you are en route to heaven.

ଓ *What mysteries in your life do you find perplexing? Talk to Mary about them.*

Praying for Sinners
Our Lady of Lourdes

February 11

My child, most people associate Lourdes, France, with healing waters, the rosary, and the Immaculate Conception. Sadly, many overlook the main purpose of my visits there—to urge everyone to pray and do penance for the conversion of sinners. I have the identical message for you, dear one.

My heart aches for my children who continue to disregard God's laws, harming others and themselves. They are teetering on the edge of a deep pit. They are oblivious to the grave danger they are in—close to losing eternal life. Someone in your family or a friend of yours may be among these lost sheep. If so, I understand how you wish they would turn their life around.

My son's sacrifice needn't be in vain in their case. Pray to me for the wayward people you are concerned about—by name if possible. I will join my prayers with yours to the Father. With my help you might also perform acts of penance for their sake. Together we can work to ensure that those you care for are saved. I look forward to tenderly embracing all of you in the next world.

ର Talk to Mary about how you can respond to her request.

Childlike Trust

February 12

My child, Jesus taught that unless you are like children, you won't enter heaven.[5] One endearing quality of little children is trust. They do as their parents tell them and believe what their parents say without question. As I lived the life God's planned for me, at times I didn't understand what was happening or why. I had to trust my heavenly Father all my life.

Believe me, the good God has planned out every facet of your life carefully and wisely. After all, he made you, he knows how many hairs are on your head, and he loves you with infinite love. God is most trustworthy.

I assure you that you can also trust me. I will be there for you both when your road to heaven is smooth and when it is rocky and treacherous. When you are beset with trials, confused, or sad, let your first thought be to speak to me. Confide to me the secrets of your heart. Cast your problems into my hands. I'm always ready to come to your aid, dear child. Trust your heavenly mother never to let go of your hand.

ଷ *Tell Mary how you would like to grow in trust of God.*

---

[5] Matthew 18:3

Hidden Deeds

February 13

My child, there is spiritual value in keeping your good deeds secret and not talking about them, or worse, boasting. The Gospels record only one act of charity I performed after Jesus was born: helping to provide wine at a wedding in Cana. In fact, the miracle of wine is the only good deed of Jesus mentioned before his public ministry. Of course, we two often did things for others during those thirty hidden years. I don't mind that you are unaware of them because of the promise Jesus repeatedly made: "Your Father who sees in secret will reward you."[6]

I, your mother, too, know when you have done a wonderful thing—made a large donation, loaned a precious possession, or did a difficult favor. I'm proud of you for it. Imagine me clapping for you! You might be tempted to announce your goodness. Resist. Be modest and avoid seeking praise and admiration. Offer your good deed to me as a secret gift. That would delight me. Instead of putting yourself on a pedestal, stay by my side.

ℭ *Do you know people who accomplished a great deed without a lot of fanfare? Ask Mary to help you imitate them.*

---

[6] Matthew 6:4

God's Love

February 14

My child, reflect with me a little while on the tremendous love God has for you. Before you were born, God loved you. From millions of possibilities, it was you he called into being. Your heavenly Father gave you a beautiful and astonishing planet as your home. His original intent was to live with you and pour out his love on you for all eternity. When sin dashed those dreams, he allowed his Son to become a human being and suffer the most atrocious death — all for love of you! Now, God reaches out to you through sacraments, especially the Eucharist. Through them God supports you on your pilgrimage back to him.

Let's not forget one undeniable sign of God's love for you: God appointed me your spiritual mother. His love flows through me to you. You enjoy the peace and comfort of my presence as I watch over you today and all the days of your life. I relish this intimate role of mine and consider it an honor. Why? Because I too love you with all my heart — more than you can ever imagine.

ℭ *Recall with Mary particular gifts of love God has bestowed on you.*

Being Needed

February 15

My child, when God needed a mother for his Son, he chose me. Most of my life was devoted to caring for Jesus and Joseph. I saw that they were clothed and fed, and I made our house a cozy home. I raised Jesus and taught him the same things your mother taught you: how to talk, walk, and pray. God needed someone to care for you, so he made me your heavenly mother. I look at you with eyes full of love, the same way I looked at Jesus.

Like me, you are responsible for meeting the needs of people God deliberately put into your life. First and foremost, these are your family members. Do your best to provide for them physically, emotionally, and spiritually. Then there are your relatives, friends, as well as complete strangers who depend on you.

Sometimes the demands made on you are overwhelming. When you tire and falter, I'm here to offer a lifeline. Feel free to ask me to help care for your loved ones and friends. Leave them in my hands. I will be glad to be your invisible partner. Let me mother you, dear.

ɔ *Talk to Mary about a person who needs assistance.*

A New Day

February 16

My child, each morning when you awake, a whole new day stretches before you. Thank God for this gift. I thank God too, for it is another opportunity for me to act as your loving mother. You never know what surprises the next hours will hold. I always hope that as you journey through the day, wonderful things await you. I want the sun to shine on you and people to smile at you. I want you to enjoy whatever you will be doing, and, most of all, I want you to stay close to God and to me. May you sense our presence enveloping you with love.

Naturally, during the day you might run across problems, if not crises. When things go wrong, remember I am with you. During these stormy patches, my arm will hold you steady so you do not collapse. Together we will wade through treacherous waters safely one step at a time. Then you will remain calm and peaceful.

With hindsight you may realize that what you thought were hardships were actually blessings. No matter how mysterious our heavenly Father's plans, trust in our love for you.

ᘓ *What do you anticipate your next day will be like? Tell Mary and ask her to be with you.*

In Times of Panic

February 17

My child, are you petrified by some frightening event or circumstance? Maybe you are losing sleep because you can't pay your debts, you face an upcoming surgery, or you live in a violent neighborhood. You might almost be paralyzed with fear. That was my experience after Joseph woke me up and told me that Herod sought to kill Jesus. My heart was pounding at the news, and I broke out in a sweat. I nervously packed. As we fled to Egypt, I held Jesus close and kept glancing back to see if Herod's soldiers were in pursuit. When Jesus was an adult and I received word that he was arrested, my heart almost stopped. So I understand your terror and dread.

As your mother, I want to spare you such horrible feelings. If you are desperate, if you think there is no one to turn to put a stop to your devastating predicament, remember to think of me. Whenever something threatens you, call upon me. You will hear me say to you over and over, "Courage, my child. I am here." You will feel me holding you close to my heart. Gradually peace will settle over you and hope will be born in you.

ଙ୍ଗ *Are there any fears currently plaguing you? Tell Mary about them.*

———

Sheer Faith

February 18

My child, you may wish for a miracle or a vision to more firmly believe in God. But faith cannot depend on solid proofs, or it wouldn't be faith! An apocryphal Gospel contains fantastic tales about our journey to Egypt. In the city where we stayed, supposedly an idol's statue crashed to the ground. At baby Jesus' command, palm trees bent to offer their fruit. I didn't need signs like these to convince me that Jesus was divine. I took God's word for it, and so should you. Remember that Jesus once berated religious leaders for asking for signs that he was the Messiah.[7]

Jesus called blessed those who believe with seeing. I agree with you that this is difficult, but it is vitally important. That is why I worry when I see you wrestling with doubts and longing for proofs. I want your faith to grow stronger every day. Pray to me, the mother of believers, that your flame of faith is never extinguished but burns steadily in your heart. I will ask my son to grant you the grace to believe in him and in his teachings. With my help, you will be blessed beyond all your expectations.

ଓଡ଼ *Talk to Mary about your questions regarding the faith.*

---

[7] Matthew 12:38–39

Hospitality

February 19

My child, both you and I are moved by refugees. Some of them abandon their homelands and possessions to save their lives. They may be ill, worn out, and poor. I can identify with these desperate people. When Jesus, Joseph, and I fled to Egypt, both along the way and in our new country we depended on the kindness of strangers. Hospitality was a high priority for our ancestors like Abraham, and I pray that you as well are cultivating a welcoming heart, open to all.

When you can take action to protect refugees coming to your country, do so. When you have the opportunity to make newcomers feel at home, grab it. As you welcome these apprehensive brothers and sisters of yours, you may be welcoming my son in disguise. Both of us would be proud of you and grateful. You might practice being hospitable by inviting people to your house for a meal or a party and treating them like royalty.

Someday you may be a refugee or at least a "foreigner" in a new neighborhood, parish, or workplace. Never fear. You will not be alone, for my heart will always be a haven for you.

ⳁ *Ask Mary to help you cheer someone up by hospitality.*

In the Face of Criticism

February 20

My child, you will never please everyone. No doubt, at times people have found fault with your personality, your clothing, your actions, and your work. Whether they informed you of their assessment in a gentle or a cruel manner, it stings. Honest criticism, though, can be beneficial. Taking it to heart can lead you to improve and be a better person. Sometimes, however, people criticize out of meanness or jealousy. If you are a victim of this, ask me to help you develop a tough skin so that their painful remarks bounce right off you. My son was the object of fierce criticism from our religious leaders, no less. That did not stop him from carrying out his mission. If you are criticized unjustly, imitate Jesus. Just ignore it.

My dear child, look to me to help you discern what is valuable criticism and then accept it with grace and humility and learn from it. When you are the target of hurtful, unfair criticism, take shelter in me, knowing that I see you and love you exactly as you are.

&cx; *Talk to Mary about criticisms you experienced, both good and bad.*

February 21 on p. 228

The Word through the Word
February 22

My child, Jesus is the living Word of God. I heard him speak personally every day when we lived together. Later I often listened to him as he taught the crowds. My son speaks to you in several ways. One in particular is the Bible. When you read Sacred Scripture, God is speaking personally to you. You come to know and love him as I do.

Be careful, dear, not to read the Bible only to acquire information. Read it slowly, thoughtfully, and prayerfully as you would a love letter from God, for that is what he intends it to be. God's word is powerful. It can transform you just like the sun gradually changes you when you are exposed to its rays. Scripture can make you ever more in love with my Jesus — something I desire for you with all my heart.

When you read the Bible with an open mind and an open heart, you will be surprised. While you read, I'm right there at your elbow. I can acquire two graces for you: the grace to understand puzzling passages and the grace to hear God's special message for you. Ask me to.

ଔ *What are you favorite Scripture verses? Explain to Mary why they appeal to you.*

Why Be Envious?

February 23

My child, from our modest home in Nazareth, I could have envied families who lived in palatial houses, wore the finest robes, and dined on delicacies. As a woman, I could have envied men their special privileges and power. But God arranged my life exactly as he wished, and so I was content.

Our good Father created you wisely and oversees the circumstances and details of your life. I would like you to be at peace knowing that everything is according to his plan. Avoid wishing you were like someone who is richer, brighter, or more charismatic than you. Don't even yearn for the spiritual gifts others possess. You have your own.

Envy erodes happiness and makes you resentful. If you harbor it, you only limp through life, sad and upset. Pray to me that you are not blind to the many good things you do possess. I will help you see clearly and be thankful for what God has graciously given you. For one thing, you have me, your mother whose love wraps you like a cloak. What more could you wish for?

ꙮ *Talk to Mary about your gratitude for who you are and what you have.*

God's Hand in the Universe
February 24

My child, you in your century know much more than I did about the magnificence of the universe. Still, on hot nights when we slept on the roof, I would gaze in wonder at the beauty of the sky bedazzled with twinkling stars. With no electric lights, our land was clothed in inky darkness. Myriads of stars were visible and seemed so close I could almost touch them. I would think about God's promise to Abraham that he would have as many descendants as the stars and through one of them all nations would be blessed. I prayed for the Messiah to come. Little did I know that I would be the one to bring him into the world!

When you behold the night sky, may it proclaim to you the might and wisdom of God who created everything in it and beyond. I pray that your heart will never fail to swell with awe and gratitude. May the stars remind you that my son redeemed all creation including you. I was happy to cooperate in salvation, and I would do it all over again for your sake, my precious one.

ぐ *Pray Psalm 8 and then share with Mary what in nature speaks to you about God's power and goodness.*

Too Busy?

February 25

My child, some days you are buried under mountains of work and wonder how you are ever going to get everything done. It pains me to see you stressed instead of calmly enjoying your precious gift of life. Your heavenly Father doesn't want you to live that way either. When you feel that you don't have time to breathe, you are inclined to skip your prayers. If you are too busy to pray, you are too busy!

I'd advise you to relieve your workload by saying no to some projects or by delegating jobs. If this is impossible, squeeze a few moments in your schedule to ask me to help you manage your time and accomplish your tasks efficiently and well. You might find that in some inexplicable way, time stretches for you!

I would do anything to ensure that you, my dear, live a happy, healthy life free from undue pressure, unreasonable burdens, and the tension headaches they bring on. Because I love you and because I have limitless spiritual resources, you can rely on me to be one of your best assistants.

ℛ *If your workload is too heavy or threatens to become so, talk it over with Mary.*

Madonna

February 26

My child, madonna, which is Italian for "my lady," refers to images that depict me alone. It has also become one of my titles. I prefer artwork that shows me with Jesus, for it is because of him that I am honored. Besides, I love my son immensely. Be assured that just as I love Jesus, I love you, my dear child in the faith. It would please me if someone painted a picture or sculpted a statue of the two of us together. In it I would be standing with my arm around you. We would be gazing at each other lovingly.

I don't mind if you call me Madonna, as long as you realize that I'm much more than your "lady"; I am your mother. Through my yes to God, your supernatural life was restored. Now I protect you from all harm, hear your pleas for help, and intercede for you before the throne of God. My dream for you is that someday you will live with me and Jesus forever. Our family in heaven will not be complete without you.

ༀ *Look up some madonnas and contemplate one of the images. Let Mary know how it makes you feel about her.*

The Light of Christ
Our Lady of Light

February 27

My child, in the eighteenth century I appeared to a woman in Italy, and asked to be honored by the title Most Holy Mother of Light. Why? Because I am the mother of Jesus, who called himself the light of the world. To be in darkness physically is frightening and dangerous. When you can't see, you might hurt yourself: walk into a door, stumble over shoes, or drive into a tree. Darkness metaphorically refers to ignorance or the state of sin. Those spiritual kinds of darkness are also dangerous. How I wish you would never be lost in them!

My son dispelled the darkness that once covered the world. He taught truth and released a flood of grace. Please stay near Jesus where his light will illumine your mind, cast out sin, and warm your heart.

I reflect the radiant light of my son like the moon reflects the sun's light. Walk within the ambit of my light wherever your life takes you — through sunlit valleys or across patches of darkness. I will keep you safe on earth and for eternity. Moreover, you too will shine to all those who see you.

ᘒ *Reveal to Mary where you need light. Ask her to provide it.*

Mary and Non-Christians

February 28

My child, you may be surprised to learn that the Qur'an, Islam's sacred scripture, has more verses about me than the Bible. One chapter is even named for me. Muslims honor me as the mother of Jesus, who to them is a great prophet of Allah and second only to Muhammad. They view me as the holiest woman and believe in my immaculate conception and the virgin birth. Muslims are my children too, as are people of every race and nation. Am I not called Queen of the Universe?

How I wish all my children would get along. One way you can return the deep love and favor I show to you is by acting to fulfill my wish. Find out what people of other faith traditions believe by reading about them and attending lectures. Better still, speak to them personally and seek common ground. Help heal my heart that aches to see good people at odds with one another. With your assistance, maybe one day I will rejoice to see all the people our heavenly Father created stream into heaven.

ଔ *Talk to Mary about your feelings concerning Muslims and other non-Christians.*

From Death into Life

February 29, Leap year

My child, as you age, you will be going to more funerals. This may evoke thoughts of death and your own mortality. Do you fear death? I would like to quell that fear. By dying, Jesus made eternal life possible for everyone. Now you can view death not as a final end to life, something to be dreaded, but a door leading you to the glorious new form of life that God originally planned for us.

I hope you have a happy death, one where you are ready to meet God. At this crucial moment, I will show myself your mother. If the evil one tries to capture your soul in a last-ditch effort, I will fight vigorously for you. I will plead to God for your salvation. You remind me of this in every Hail Mary when you ask me to pray for you at the hour of your death.

In whatever form death comes to you, don't worry, I will be right there at your side to usher you into the next world with a radiant smile on my face in anticipation of our eternal life together.

ଯ *Does the thought of your death make you afraid? Tell Mary about it. Pray a Hail Mary.*

March

Cherishing Memories

March 1

My child, Scripture mentions two events in Jesus' life that I "treasured in my heart": hearing the shepherds' account of the angels announcing his birth and finding him as a boy in "his Father's house," speaking with the teachers in the Temple. Imagine how many other events I pondered and treasured—my wedding to the bewildered but trusting Joseph; the day Jesus first said, "Mama"; Jesus hugging me good-bye as he left home to begin his ministry; and his visit to me as the risen, glorified Lord.

Our good God is at work in your life no less than he was at work in mine. Reflect on moments when you felt his loving presence, maybe through a little "miracle." What happened? How did you feel? What were the results? Unlike women at my time, you can read and write. Nourish your prayer life by recording your spiritual highpoints so you don't forget them. Occasionally read them over and thank God for them. I will be with you, joining my thanks to yours. Write down, too, times you felt exceptionally close to me. Recalling them will remind you of the tender love I bear for you.

☙ *Talk to Mary about a special memory you have.*

When Forgiving Seems Impossible

March 2

My child, atop a Nazareth hill are the ruins of an old chapel named Our Lady of the Fright. Tradition holds that this site is where I stood watching a mob try to throw my son off a cliff on Mount Precipice. That bloodthirsty mob was composed of our neighbors and relatives. Jesus escaped, but I had to return to our village and live with those people who tried to kill him.

Daily as I drew water from the well and shopped at the market, I endured people's whispers, curious looks, and sometimes cruel remarks. No doubt, you've been in a similar situation. You rub shoulders at work with someone who offended you. At a social event, you are seated with a man or woman who dislikes you. You have to bite your tongue when someone praises a person who insulted or criticized you. Jesus taught us to love enemies—a huge challenge when our instinct is to take revenge. One step toward loving forgiveness is to pray for your enemies.

I had the grace to forgive my neighbors. I'd like to obtain that grace for you too. Just ask. Then the hard part of your heart will soften and the peace I wish for you, dear, will be complete.

ɔঽ *Is there someone you find hard to forgive? Talk to Mary about this.*

The Value of Work

March 3

My child, although Genesis presents work as punishment for sin, actually to work is to be like God, the master craftsman who made all creation. You find fulfillment in it. We, the holy family, were not exempt from work. Joseph and Jesus were engaged in construction work, hard manual labor, while I did the household tasks of cooking, cleaning, and sewing, and other menial chores.

In the course of this day, you will carry out any number of jobs, major and trivial. No matter what you labor at, do it cheerfully and to the best of your ability. No cutting corners! As you toil, I will be alongside of you, bolstering your strength, confidence, or inspiration.

Like my work, yours is a share in God's continuing creation, your contribution to the world, and the furtherance of God's kingdom. Make your work more meaningful by offering it to God through my hands. As though through alchemy, I will turn it into something even more precious, gilding it with gold. When your work becomes a gift to God, you will discover more joy in it and you will be blessed for it.

Ꮬ *Do you enjoy your job, or do you find it difficult? Speak with Mary about your attitude toward your work.*

Penance

March 4

My child, penance is seldom mentioned or practiced today, except as an assignment after the Sacrament of Reconciliation. When I visited at Fatima, one message I gave was, "Penance, penance, penance." I say the same to you today, dear one. Why? Because penance develops self-control, atones for sin, and wins graces. It draws you closer to me and Jesus.

You needn't go about in camel skins and live on locusts and honey as my cousin John the Baptist did. You don't have to wear a hairshirt or whip yourself with cords as some ascetic saints did. Little acts like letting other people have their way, tackling a job you'd rather not do, and resisting another slice of pizza can be just as meritorious . . . and as painful. Accepting your daily crosses gracefully is an excellent practice of penance.

As you plan to incorporate penance in your life, ask me to inspire you. And when you perform penance, don't do it in a heavy, plodding way, but with a light heart. Think of it as a sure pathway to eternal glory and to me, who eagerly awaits you.

ભ *Talk to Mary about the penances she experienced and some of yours.*

Listening to Jesus

March 5

My child, at the wedding in Cana, when the wine ran out, I knew I could depend on my son to help. I told the servers, "Do whatever he tells you." I repeat them to you. When you do what Jesus says, expect wonders. Jesus told the waiters to fill the jars with water. Those men had good reason to ignore him or laugh at him. Wine was needed, not water. Besides, what would a carpenter know about making wine? Still, the waiters obeyed, and so the wine flowed and everyone was happy.[8]

I know Jesus sometimes asks difficult or seemingly outrageous things of you. You wonder if you have the stamina, intelligence, faith, or love to comply. You'd rather just slink away and pretend you didn't hear. But because I love you, I say, "Don't!" What my son asks is always for the best. Trust me to be hovering over you with motherly concern as you attempt to carry out his orders. When you obey Jesus, you might be surprised at the outcome. In any case, I guarantee that you too will be happy, if not here, in heaven.

ଔ *Is Jesus telling you to do something that you find challenging? Talk to his mother about it.*

---

[8] John 2:1–11

Tower of David

March 6

My child, in the Litany of Loreto, you invoke me as Tower of David. A tower serves as a lookout and a protection for a town. The Tower of David mentioned in the Bible[9] was covered with a thousand shields. By calling on me as the Tower of David, you acknowledge that I am your strong defense. As fiercely as a lioness protects her cub, I will protect you from any evil person or dangerous thing that threatens you.

As you strive to live as our loving God desires, you battle three enemies: the world, the flesh, and the devil. Original sin left you weak and prone to sin, but I, your mother, am powerful, even more powerful than St. Michael the Archangel. You do not need to fear the devil because I trod that serpent underfoot. With me as your ally, Satan will not be able to take you prisoner.

No matter how often you struggle against temptation, I will come to your rescue. As soon as you pray a Hail Mary or simply call my name, I will be there to defend you. I protected Jesus, and I will protect you.

ᘓ *Talk to Mary about your usual temptations. Pray the Litany of Loreto.*

---

[9] Song of Solomon 4:4

Destructive Moping

March 7

My child, I'm sorry when you meet up with ugly and painful experiences: failures, disappointments, and tragedies. They are part of every person's life, mine included if you recall. You can sink into depression if you dwell on your misfortunes and injustices done to you. I certainly wouldn't want that to happen to you, dear. Ask me to help you blot your problems out of your mind, shift the focus of your thoughts from yourself to other people, and move forward in peace and hope. Try not to talk about your problems, in particular, if that involves tarnishing someone's reputation. True, venting might afford you some relief and satisfaction, but it spreads your dark cloud over your listeners.

Trust that our all-good God in his mysterious way draws good out of bad situations. Remember that the horror of the cross led to glory for Jesus, me, and the whole human race. Your crosses might actually be graces.

I remind you of the blessings God has showered on you. You are alive, you have family and friends, you are destined for eternal life, and you have a heavenly mother who is always available to you and who loves you more than words can tell. Smile and be happy, child!

෮ *Share with Mary some of the positive things about your life.*

Fidelity

March 8

My child, God is always faithful to his promises and faithful to you. The good God and I both love you no matter what. Our love is everlasting and unconditional. Likewise, you are to be faithful to your promises to God. I witnessed your baptismal commitment to reject sin, the works of God's enemy Satan, and to live as God's child. I resolved to help you keep your promise.

To be true to my agreement to live as God's handmaid, I had to surmount numerous obstacles. Thanks to God's grace I remained faithful. On your journey to heaven, you encounter cliffs, chasms, and storms that tempt you to reconsider your promises to God and break them. Voices urge you to stray from the right path. However, you have at your disposal the same graces that empowered me. You have merely to ask me and I will obtain them for you. With my help, you will not be unfaithful to God. Neither will you be a lukewarm Christian but one on fire with love of God and others. You will be worthy of God's promises, and I will be very proud of you.

ଛ *Talk to Mary about your desire to be faithful to God.*

Mary's Legacy

March 9

My child, the legacy I left you is the beautiful pattern of my life. By following in my footsteps and holding tightly onto my hand, you will be pleasing to God. Three of my acts in particular I recommend. First, listen to God however he speaks, and do what he asks, as I did on the day I consented to his plan for me. Second, have a heart brimming with love. My love for God compelled me to say yes to him even though I didn't know the consequences. My love for others had me hasten to Elizabeth's house and later to Jesus at a wedding in order to spare newlyweds embarrassment. Third, trust God implicitly no matter what, even when sorrow overwhelms you or when unbearable and unexplainable circumstances occur. On Calvary I trusted even though my son's appalling death was excruciating for me and seemed to make no sense.

When you imitate me, you imitate Jesus and will be recognized as my child. How happy it would make me if when Jesus meets you at heaven's gates he exclaims, "Come in. You remind me so much of my mother." Remember: listen, love, and trust.

ℭ *Make plans with Mary to imitate her today in some way.*

Close to Jesus

March 10

My child, what a privilege it was to share so many of my days on earth with Jesus! He longs to share the days of your life too. I know him better than anyone else does, and I also know you through and through. Because I am your mother who cares deeply about you, I desire that you draw nearer to my son and strengthen your relationship with him. That way your life will be filled with the meaning and happiness you crave. I'd like to offer you some motherly advice.

I urge you to be aware of Jesus' presence day and night. His loving gaze is always upon you. Bask in his love, and now and then speak with him. Unite with him frequently in Holy Communion, when in the form of food and drink he becomes closer to you than anyone can ever be. If you disappoint Jesus by sinning, rise up and go to him quickly. He is merciful and will always pardon you. Look on people as other Christs and love him in them. Let your passionate devotion to Jesus compel you to bring others to know him as you do.

Lastly, stay close to me, his blessed mother, for then you will surely remain close to Jesus.

ભ *Talk to Mary about your relationship with her son and how you might deepen it.*

A Burning Bush

March 11

My child, God came to Moses at a bush that was on fire but was not consumed. The bush remained whole. This burning bush is a symbol of me, for God revealed himself to the world through me, miraculously leaving my virginity intact.

I like to think that the burning bush also signifies my intense, undying love for our heavenly Father. My prayer for you is that you remain close to me. That way flames of love from me will leap to you, and you will catch on fire. How I wish you would burn steadily with love for God and zeal for making him known and loved!

I will help you stoke that fire when the storms you inevitably encounter threaten to extinguish it. Together we will keep that love aflame in your heart. We will see that it spreads to others you meet along the way, enveloping them in light and warmth. Then someday, my beloved child, you will behold the shining glory of God in all of his splendor and be totally engulfed in the flames of his mighty, incredible love.

ལ *How can you make God known and loved especially by people who need the warmth of his love? Ask Mary to enlighten you.*

Misinterpretations

March 12

My child, it is easy to jump to wrong conclusions. Once when Jesus was preaching, relatives and I went to see him. Someone informed Jesus that we were waiting, but he replied, "My mother and my brothers are those who hear the word of God and do it."[10] At first I was embarrassed at this apparent rebuff. Then I realized that of course Jesus included us with those who do God's will.

I want to save you from making the same mistake, for it only leads to sorrow. When someone's remark sounds harsh and hurtful, be careful not to misinterpret it. Or when you observe a person who appears to be doing something suspicious, don't assume they are doing wrong. Families and friendships can be destroyed that way. Give people the benefit of the doubt. You might consider the bond between you. Unknown circumstances may have prompted the questionable words or actions. Ask for an explanation. Often words can be taken two ways. Choose the more positive interpretation. Look on other people the way I look on you — with love and understanding.

℘ *Talk to Mary about a misunderstanding you experienced and the path to reconciliation.*

---

[10] Luke 8:21

Near to Mary

March 13

My child, one of the most frightening events in my life was losing Jesus in Jerusalem. Joseph and I had assumed he was with us in the caravan. It was three long days before we discovered Jesus in the Temple. You can imagine what those days—and especially the nights—were like for me. Not only had I lost my son, but I had lost the world's Messiah!

You also are very dear to me, precious child. I would hate to lose you! Probably one or more of your close friends for apparently no reason cut ties and disappeared from your life. If so, you know how that can hurt. I wouldn't like that to happen to us. With all my heart I want to stay friends with you for your whole life.

Please keep in touch with me. Think of me often. You might keep my picture in your wallet as a reminder. Talk to me about all the details of your days. I won't be bored, and I'm a good listener. Read about me so you get to know me better. And celebrate my feasts in a special way. Doing all of these things will keep our relationship alive and healthy. You will not move away from me, and I promise that I will never distance myself from you.

 CR *Assure Mary that you would like your relationship with her to grow stronger daily.*

Love in Action

March 14

My child, when you see a crisis unfolding, do you wait for someone else to step up to help? Do you freeze and waste time considering whether you should do something? If you are a true child of mine, you will spring into action. Remember what I did at the Cana wedding. When the wine ran out, I approached Jesus and jumpstarted his public life.

I will also help you to be alert for occasions when assistance is needed. When a woman in a wheelchair is having a hard time maneuvering, when someone balancing boxes is approaching a door, when you hear, "Are there any volunteers?" make the first move. Don't stop to think. Act spontaneously and trust God for the outcome. Are you afraid that you are too shy to act the part of a hero or a good Samaritan? Don't forget—I'm always at hand to prompt and embolden you.

After performing a good deed, erase it from your mind. Above all, don't draw attention to it. After Jesus supplied wine, I didn't go around telling the other guests that I had saved the day. Let your deed be a secret between you and me.

ଔ *Did a person ever come to your rescue? How did you feel? Tell Mary about it.*

Short Prayers

March 15

My child, to stay in touch with me, you needn't pray long, complicated prayers out of a book. You don't even have to talk with me informally about whatever is on your mind. I do enjoy and cherish those conversations, but I understand that some days you are very busy and long prayers are a luxury. I'd like to suggest another and simpler way to pray. Intersperse the moments of your day with short aspirations like "My Mother, my hope" and "Our Lady, Queen of Peace, pray for us." This will bring us together. Just a single word like "Mary" or "Mother" will do. Consider the quick responses when someone shouts, "Fire!"

You might pray traditional aspirations or make them up yourself. Being contacted by a relative or a dear friend delights you. It can make your day. I experience the same joy when I hear from you, my dear child. It means that you are thinking about me and care enough to spend time connecting with me. You are always on my mind, every minute of each day, but especially when you call upon me. Then I give you my full attention.

ob *Plan with Mary some aspirations you will pray.*

Resembling Your Mother

March 16

My child, Jesus greatly resembled me. His eyes, nose, and mouth were replicas of mine. At times I noticed a mannerism in him that I recognized as my own. It made me smile. Naturally no other son so closely looked like his mother. All of Jesus' DNA was from me!

You are my child too, and I wish for you to be like me as much as possible — of course, not physically but spiritually. As you strive to live as a Christian, a follower of Jesus, take me as your model and study my qualities: faithfulness, humility, charity. Then you will also be like Jesus. This will not be difficult, for I'm always at your side to assist you, urge you on, and pray for you.

Married couples who have grown old together often look like each other. Their deep love and shared life caused this. How wonderful it would be if your love for Jesus and me would result in your becoming like us. Spend as much time in our company as you can. Then people who see you and the saintly way you act might be prompted to think of us.

ભ *Talk to Mary about one of her characteristics you would like to cultivate.*

Gentle as a Dove

March 17

My child, I'm known as a sweet and gentle woman. I admit, though, it was a challenge to maintain my composure when people unintentionally or even deliberately were unkind to me. When a woman squeezed in front of me in the line at a market stall, I felt like rebuking her. When a neighbor criticized Jesus, it was all I could do not to respond to the rude person with a stinging retort. But with God's grace, I managed to restrain myself.

So I understand how difficult it is for you not to explode with rage when someone provokes you. When you are the victim of a snide remark or when someone cuts you off in traffic, you might see red. At such times, turn to me for help in keeping your temper in leash. Making a person feel bad by retaliating with a hurtful comment or action only multiplies evil. In addition, it lays the weight of guilt on you. If you remain calm, you too will gain the reputation of being gentle and kind. Moreover, your life will go more smoothly, which is what I wish for you, my dear.

ↂ *Ask Mary to help you imitate her gentleness in the face of any provocation.*

Dark Days

March 18

My child, I'm compared to the beautiful, serene moon, whose brightness is a reflection of the sun, a giant ball of fire. This analogy is a fitting because all of my glory is simply a reflection of God's magnificent light. Similarly, your goodness is God shining in and through you.

The moon is brightest on nights that are the darkest. I'm aware that you have your share of dark days. That is the stark reality of life. Tragedies befall you and your loved ones. You experience disappointment, failure, and maybe even persecution. On some days trials beset you from all sides, and you don't see any end to them.

It's during those trying times, that I am most willing, in fact, eager, to illuminate your path to safety and renewed joy. Lift your head and raise your eyes to me. I will be swift to relieve you of your troubles and lighten your spirits. That is what mothers do. I, your heavenly mother, am more devoted to you than any earthly mother has ever been to her child.

ᴄ₰ *Express your gratitude to Mary for her loving help. Tell her how you will depend on her during future troubles.*

A Soulmate
Joseph, Husband of Mary

March 19

My child, God was so good to choose Joseph to be my husband, my partner. Joseph sacrificed a normal marriage to help me fulfill my challenging role. This kind man of integrity was my best friend. He accepted my son as his own. He protected Jesus and me and worked hard to support us. It was a joy to cook for Joseph, wash his clothes, and sit quietly with him in the evenings. We loved each other deeply.

You must have someone who means a lot to you — a spouse, a sibling, or a good friend. This soulmate shares your life, gives you good advice, keeps your secrets, does favors, and lets you cry on his or her shoulder. Such a person knows all about you, including your faults, and likes you anyway. As I thanked God often for my Joseph, thank God for sending someone to you who will grow old with you and brighten and lighten your days.

In case you haven't realized it, the description of a soulmate applies to me in my relationship with you! Heart and soul I am dedicated to being your loving companion through all the ups and downs of your life.

℣ *Tell Mary about your soulmate and ask her to pray for him or her.*

Are You Lonely?

March 20

My child, I'm sure you feel lonely sometimes. Perhaps on a grey, rainy day you sit at home alone, or at a gathering everyone around you is chatting to someone, but no one is speaking with you. Being by yourself can make you sad and sorry for yourself. After Joseph died and Jesus left home, I was alone for a few years. I missed them sorely and sometimes imagined I heard their voices. I would recall happier times like when Jesus proudly showed me the first object he made from wood and when Joseph's face shone with love for me.

One cure for loneliness is to reach out to someone else who might be feeling lonely. That is what I did in Nazareth to perk up my spirits. I visited the new widow, and I brought fresh honey bread to the sick woman down the street.

When loneliness takes hold of you, remember that you are not really completely alone. I am there with you, longing to speak with you, and so is Jesus. In fact, the Trinity dwells in the innermost of your being. Be aware of us and talk to us, darling. Let me cheer you up by reminding you of my love for you.

ଔ *Talk to Mary about what you can do when you are lonely.*

Who Are You to Judge?

March 21

My child, Jesus said, "Do not judge, and you will not be judged."[11] You tend to judge people automatically because your moral compass alerts you when something is wrong. Jesus did not mean that nothing is immoral. He was warning against wrong kinds of judgment.

You might judge someone to be sinful or flawed hypocritically when you possess the identical fault—or worse! Or you might judge without knowing all the facts, such as the motive or the alleged culprit's background. You might judge out of a sense of self-righteousness. You feel good that you are not guilty of the same fault. Another incorrect way to judge is doing it fairly but harshly. Ask me to preserve you from unloving, unchristian ways of judging that would mar your character.

Consider how I judged people. For instance, I knew that Peter had betrayed my son, but I understood his weakness and fear and forgave him. Judge people the way you would like to be judged, dear. Put yourself in their shoes. When you make mistakes, I always judge you with a healthy dose of love.

ℭℛ *Talk to Mary about times you were wrongly judged.*

---

[11] Luke 6:37

Perseverance

March 22

My child, you have set several commendable goals for yourself, and for that I congratulate you. Of course, the loftiest goal is reaching heaven. Some days you walk lightly and joyfully toward this goal. You are full of enthusiasm and ambition. Then there are days when your spirits flag. The way is strewn with problems. You are working so hard, but there is little progress. You see others achieving far more than you with not as much effort. You are discouraged and trudge heavily along the way. Eventually you grow tired and want nothing more than to sink down on the ground and quit.

I, dear one, am on the sidelines, rooting for you, coaching you, and urging you not to give up. Turn to me for help and lean on me. I will be like a sturdy staff supporting you. I can win for you a spurt of energy that will see you through to the finish line. Keep your eyes on me and you will achieve the only reward that really matters, eternal life.

℘ *Share with Mary any hurdles you see in your life today.*

Foiled Wishes

March 23

My child, not everything always goes the way you want it to. You can fuss and fume about this until you give yourself a headache and upset everyone around you. Or you can gracefully accept the inevitable as God's holy will. Make his will your will. This is the better course for you. God is far wiser than you, and he wants only what is good. So trust him as I did when I was abruptly asked to change my marriage plans.

I will help you get through the frustrating period when your will is thwarted. I remind you that God tests people like gold in a crucible. You may emerge stronger for the experience. Surrender to your heavenly Father and leave him free to work.

In your distress, take refuge in my arms while I pray that God grant you a surge of faith to go on with your life calmly and confidently. Know that my love and care for you are always within reach, sweetheart. Let me soothe your furrowed brow and dry your tears.

℘ *Talk to Mary about happenings in your life that you find distressing.*

What's the Rush?

March 24

My child, often I see you running around like a frightened rabbit. You hurry through your household chores, you gobble down your food as quickly as you can, and you dash out the door to "run" errands. Life in Nazareth was not as frenetic, but then, we didn't have as much to do as you moderns. Rushing is just a habit. Would you like to try to break it? Your life will be much more pleasant if you slow down. I offer to be your anchor while the maelstrom of life whirls around you.

Sit down, be still and quiet, and look around you. Take in and savor the marvels of the world and your own family and home. Look ahead to the jobs for which you are seriously responsible. Mentally cross off your list those that are not as important. Breathe deeply and listen to me assure you that all will be done in good time. After you get up again, move slowly and at a deliberate, steady pace.

When you feel like hurrying, hear me whisper in your ear over and over like a mantra, "Peace, my child." Acting calmly will preserve your health, and I won't be so anxious about you.

ॐ Ask Mary to help slow you down so you can enjoy life more.

Open Your Heart to God
Annunciation

March 25

My child, when the Angel Gabriel announced that I would bear the Son of God who would rule an everlasting kingdom, I was stunned. He explained that although I was a virgin, the Holy Spirit would bring about this Incarnation. Spontaneously I consented to this unprecedented proposal. I didn't stop to think, but gave myself over to what was God's pleasure. It never crossed my mind to consult my parents or Joseph. The messenger was not much help. He simply vanished.

When it comes to listening to God's will for you, no matter how daunting the prospect, take me as your model. Make your heart like mine. Submit to God with an open mind, an open heart, and open arms. An angel is not likely to carry a message to you, but God will speak in other ways, perhaps quietly in your innermost being. Be attuned to his voice every day. You mustn't fear the consequences of saying yes, for I have a deep reservoir of love for you. The graces I obtain for you will be sufficient to handle whatever the future holds.

ca *Talk to Mary about what God might be asking of you today or in the near future.*

Another Incarnation

March 26

My child, I surrendered myself to God at the Annunciation. I let him use my body and blood to become a human being. Today I urge you to surrender yourself to God so that he can continue his saving work through you. Give God your arms to reach out to feed the hungry, embrace the lonely and outcasts, and heal the hurting. Give God your feet to take you to places where people need the comfort of God's love — refugee camps, hospitals, and prisons, as well as your neighbor's house. Give God your mouth to speak words of encouragement and consolation, to promote peace, and, in particular, to declare the Good News of Jesus.

I never regretted the lifelong commitment I made to God, not even when it led to sadness and excruciating suffering. Neither will you be sorry for allowing our merciful and loving God to use you. If you should ever encounter grief and pain because of your yes to God, never fear. I will be beside you to cushion them. So be brave, my dear, and place yourself in God's hands to use as he wishes. Bring forth his love into the world.

❧ *Talk over with Mary ways God might work through you.*

Mirror of the Trinity

March 27

My child, at the Incarnation when I was united with the Holy Spirit, I was also one with the Father and the Son. These three divine Persons are inseparable. I was drawn into the intimate life of the Trinity. In a unique and beautiful way, I shared in the holiness of God and reflected it in my person.

Like me, you too, dear, are a temple of the Trinity, God's holy dwelling place. Your baptism was the source of this amazing grace. I pray that you allow God's holiness to shine out from you and do nothing to dim it. From time to time be conscious of God living within your very being. Rejoice in God's presence and draw strength from it.

I also am with you, standing at your side invisibly but truly, imploring you to deepen your relationship with God, and interceding on your behalf. As your spiritual mother, my principal goal on earth is for you to be united everlastingly with God — Father, Son, and Holy Spirit. Then my joy will be complete.

ൖ *Speak with Mary about your desire to be holy.*

Are You Bored?

March 28

My child, at times you might resent the monotony of your daily routines. You get up, eat breakfast, go to work, eat lunch, work, eat supper, relax a little, and then go to bed. Day follows day, and breaks and vacations are few and far between. You might wonder, Is this all there is to life?

In Nazareth my days were not very exciting either. I fetched water from the well, served breakfast, went to the market, ground grain, baked bread, sewed or did laundry, and prepared supper. Our entertainment was visiting with our neighbors. For most of these days, however, I had the privilege of living with Jesus and basked in his presence, so nothing actually was ever ordinary.

You don't have to be jealous of me. You too are living with Jesus. My son is always with you and within you. Make an effort to be conscious of his presence. Talk to him frequently. That way your life will never be dull. I am also your daily companion. With us walking with you, why not look on every day as an adventure?

ca *Plan with Mary how you can be more aware of her and Jesus acting in your life.*

Accepting Help

March 28

My child, do you sometimes reject a person's offer to assist you? You might reply, "No, thank you. I can do it myself" or "It's not heavy." I know you like to be independent, but allow people to help you. This is an act of charity on your part because you allow your helper to experience the good feeling that comes from being needed and useful. Besides, your helper will be rewarded for his or her kindness.

Accepting help is nothing to be ashamed of. I was definitely grateful for Joseph's help and also the advice my mother and mother-in-law gave me. Later as a widow who no longer had a child to depend on, I gladly accepted the apostle John's help.

Don't be afraid to ask people for assistance either. And, dear, whenever you are faced with a challenging task, don't tough it out and struggle alone. Ask for my help. I will never refuse you, for you are the apple of my eye. It gives me great pleasure when you beg me for favors, confident of my love for you.

଼ *Is there something you need Mary's help with today? Tell her about it and request her assistance.*

Humility

March 29

My child, Jesus values humility, a virtue in those who are honest about themselves. It's the opposite of pride, an exaggerated view of self. Being the Mother of God was a tremendous honor. I realize my admirable qualities were not my doing, but God's. At the visitation I stated, "Surely, from now on all generations will call me blessed." That may sound boastful, but immediately I acknowledged, "For the Mighty One has done great things for me."[12] I credit God for any good I do.

You, too, possess wonderful qualities and skills that make you the child I love. Remember, though, that these are gifts from our heavenly Father. He disperses them as he pleases. Your gifts do not make you better than others, only different. Avoid puffing yourself up to be greater than you are and looking down on others. Your gifts may disappear at any moment! I will pray that you see yourself as God and I see you. This true picture is beautiful enough. You needn't pretend you are more perfect. Thank God for his goodness to you.

ᗒ *Talk to Mary about one of your virtues or talents.*

---

[12] Luke 1:48–49

Fight Temptations

March 30

My child, as you travel the highway to heaven, the devil lurks waiting to waylay you and rob you of your inheritance of eternal life. I was sinless, but that doesn't necessarily mean I wasn't tempted. Even Jesus, the Son of God was tempted by Satan. I know how hard you try to resist temptation, and I love you for it. When you lose a particular battle and succumb, I don't think any less of you. I realize that you are fighting against jealous supernatural forces who desire your ruin. They are more powerful than you, but together we can foil them.

Whenever you have the urge to continue being a slave to a bad habit, to go along with someone who is pressuring you to do wrong, to harm another person by your words or action, or to sin in any other way, call on me. Say a quick Hail Mary. I, your mother, will speed to your rescue and keep you headed to your destination safely. My "fiat" at the Annunciation led to the devil's ultimate defeat, and I can conquer him for you.

ᙣ *Talk to Mary about the way Satan most often tempts you.*

Precious Water

March 31

My child, water is one of God's greatest and most abundant gifts. It's also very practical. How did you use water today—to wash, cook, clean, swim, or travel? No doubt, you've experienced the beauty of lakes, rivers, and waterfalls our heavenly Father placed on earth. Water plays an important role in your spiritual life too. Through the waters of baptism you became a Christian, my beloved child. You recall this each time you bless yourself with holy water.

With a twist of the faucet, water gushes out for you. In Nazareth there was a freshwater spring. Each morning I walked to the well and filled a bucket for the day's needs. Some of my children today do not have such easy access to clean water. I beg you not only to pray for them but to take action to remedy this situation. I count on you to perform this act of mercy, and I am confident that my son will bless you for it. By the way, once in a while remember to thank our good God for his gift of water.

ღ *Talk to Mary about what you can do to help make clean water available for all.*

April

Joy

April 1

My child, remember that you were made for joy here and hereafter. Life can hand you some troubles that you find disrupting and disheartening. But no matter how painful and serious, take comfort in knowing that they will not last forever. The sun will again break through and shine on you. You will be able to laugh again. Just be patient and trust that come what may, God is in control.

On those trying days when your joy fades, I will help you cope with the cause. Just cry out to me and hold onto my mantle with both hands. I will advise you to focus on the rich blessings our heavenly Father showers on you. You are alive, and this fantastic world is your playground. You have family and friends who cherish you. You are on track for a life of unending glory and bliss. And I remind you that you have a heavenly mother who has a vast ocean of love for you, sweetheart. These facts ought to be the source of a deep-rooted joy in your heart that no one or nothing can take from you.

ひ *Is there anything diminishing your joy today? Tell Mary about it.*

The High Road

April 2

My child, every day you face situations where you must decide to take the high road or the low road. The high road of superior morality is not an easy one. Nor is it popular. You may feel as though you are the only one on it! But don't worry. You will have a companion. I will be walking right along with you, urging you on to do the right thing and proud of you for acting with integrity.

When someone offends you or treats you unjustly, you can choose to join them on the low road and retaliate. But remember that Jesus taught his followers to turn the other cheek when someone strikes you.[13] At times you may have the opportunity to acquire something immorally and without being discovered. But by taking the high road, you will live up to your highest ideals. Even if your good choice results in pain or suffering of some kind, you will have the satisfaction and solace of knowing you acted nobly. And you will have a clear conscience. Who knows? You also might win the admiration and respect of others and inspire them to act according to high principles.

ை *Is there a situation tempting you to take the low road? Ask Mary to obtain for you the grace to choose wisely.*

---

[13] Matthew 5:39

Idols

April 3

My child, you do not worship false gods of wood and stone as people did in my time. You must be very careful, however, not to replace God with other idols popular today.

Some people center their lives on possessions and become hoarders. Some are intent on amassing as much money as they can. Ironically, in the end they will own nothing other than their good deeds. Other people ignore God as though he didn't exist and devote their lives to the pleasure of alcohol, drugs, food, or sex. Some people idolize a man or woman to the extent that they will do anything, even sin, for that person. None of these false gods bring lasting happiness, and they erode the chance for eternal happiness with the only God.

I am the mother of this true God who entrusted you to me. My fervent prayer is that you keep God snugly in the center of your heart. I will not rest until you are safe in my loving arms.

ဢ *Take an honest look at your life to see if you worship some idol. If you do, ask Mary to rescue you. If not, ask her to keep you safe.*

Thanksgiving in Advance

April 4

My child, giving thanks before receiving an answer to prayer is a sign of faith. When Jonah was in the big fish's belly, he prayed a prayer of thanksgiving.[14] The fish spewed him out on the shore. King Jehoshaphat prayed similarly when the Judeans were about to be attacked by three nations. He sent some to walk ahead of his army and sing, "Give thanks to the Lord."[15] The invading armies destroyed one another. Judah was spared.

You might not be in dire straits like Jonah and King Jehoshaphat. Certainly from time to time though, you face situations that require help. No matter what you need, ask me to help you obtain it from God. You might thank both God and me in advance for providing it for you. This will show that you have confidence in our love for you. That is why I would like to hear you say thank you before your prayers are answered. Remember to say thank you afterward too. As your earthly mother would say, "That is only good manners."

ଓ *Are you praying for some intention? Thank Mary for placing your request before God.*

---

[14] Jonah 2:9

[15] 2 Chronicles 20:21

Distractions

April 5

My child, are you concerned because as you pray, numerous distractions assail you like bothersome gnats? Maybe at the end of a period of prayer, you don't think you prayed at all! You want to be focused on God and me, and you become angry with yourself when you aren't. I assure you, distractions during prayer are natural. I understand. Your heavenly Father and I value the time you spend praying as well as the efforts you make to concentrate—even if they are futile! Our love for you does not fade. A mother still loves a child who lisps or stutters.

I do have some motherly advice. Make sure you pray in a quiet place where you are alone. Looking at a religious image as you pray might control your thoughts. Keep in mind that a distraction might be God prompting you to pray for a person or about a matter. You might weave it into your prayer.

I would be happy to assist you in praying. Just ask me. And don't fret about it when your mind wanders. You are probably praying better than you realize, darling.

ભ *How do you feel about your prayer life? Tell Mary about it.*

Newness

April 6

My child, do you find yourself in a rut, doing the same things in the same way day after day, week after week, and maybe year after year? That is dull and could be depressing. My heart's desire is for you to enjoy life to the fullest, my dear child. One way to achieve that is to introduce something new into it. My son came so you would have life in abundance,[16] but in many ways it's you who are in control of the quality of your life. As you travel through the time allotted you, it's up to you to decide to surge forward, stay stuck in place, or step backward.

Enrich your life by surprising yourself. Start a hobby, make a new friend, volunteer somewhere, learn something new, or change jobs. This will lift you out of the rut; you might even soar!

Change is difficult and intimidating, but I'm eager to help you free yourself from deadening boredom. Cling tight to my hand. I won't let you fall. I look forward to seeing your eyes sparkle again.

ख़ *Talk over with Mary a few ideas for refreshing changes to make in your life.*

---

[16] John 10:10

Growing Older

April 7

My child, everyone on earth right now, including you, is aging. That is a fact of life ever since the Fall. You see your older family members and friends turning grey, becoming feebler, falling and breaking bones, and getting sick. Entering the golden years may frighten you. You don't like the thought of your eyesight becoming dim and your hearing decreasing. You dread the idea of being dependent on others. You would like to continue to work, to go out with family and friends, and to run your own house forever.

You may wonder about your final years: whether your mental ability will decline, where you will live, and who will care for you. Put your mind at ease. From the day you were born, I have been watching over you diligently. Whether you were skipping along pleasant paths or making your way through pockets of darkness, I have walked beside you, encouraging you and praying for you. Do you think I would ever leave you, my dear, even if everyone else does? You can have absolute trust in me. I will be with you until your last breath.

ભ *Share with Mary your feelings about aging.*

Immensity of God

April 8

My child, you cannot imagine the majesty and splendor of God. You see hints in his handiwork: spectacular sunsets, magnificent oceans, and intricate dew-covered spider webs. You sense a glimmer of God's greatness and tenderness whenever you behold a newborn or experience the powerful emotion of human love. But on earth you can never fathom the glory of God the way I do in his presence. There are no words to describe the tremendous divine love that envelops us here.

Trust me. Being with almighty God is worth any price. Live by God's laws of love. Do as my son taught. Pray and sacrifice. Keep your eyes on the goal and never give up pursuing it. Do nothing to allow the brilliant future God has planned for you slip through your fingers.

Because I know God and because I know you and love you both with all of my being, I will do everything in my power to bring you together. When you doubt your ability to attain heaven, when you feel too weak or too tired to keep trying, cry out to me. I will be a good mother to you and lead you home.

ख *Ask Mary to help you through anything hindering you from your eternal goal.*

Repeating Yes

April 9

My child, saying yes to God once is not enough. After my first yes to being the mother of God, I had to repeat it over and over. Yes to going to Bethlehem, yes to helping Elizabeth, and yes to standing at the foot of the cross on Calvary. You, too, are called to say yes to God beyond the yes that committed you to him at your baptism. Sometimes you must say yes more than once during the day!

When you feel the Holy Spirit nudging you to perform an act of charity, hear me whisper, "Say yes." When your conscience tells you to ignore a temptation, hear me encourage you, "Say yes." When someone asks for a favor, hear me tell you, "Say yes." The road to heaven is paved with yeses. I will do my utmost to ensure that you take that road. Each time you nod your head yes and cheerfully recommit yourself to Jesus' way of life, you can be sure that I am smiling broadly at you and saying a heartfelt yes!

ℛ *What opportunities to say yes do you foresee? Ask Mary to help you respond as positively as she would.*

Doubts

April 10

My child, if you are normal, sometimes you are plagued with doubts about your faith. Among other things, you may wonder if the Bible is really God's Word, if Jesus truly rose from the dead, and even if God exists. Don't let doubts rattle you. Questioning can lead to a sounder faith. I was praying with the apostles in the upper room before the Holy Spirit reinforced their faith on Pentecost. As you struggle with doubts, I will be praying with you too, dear. Pray to the Holy Spirit, who is your Helper too, for enlightenment.

Your doubts are actually a good thing when they impel you to search for answers. Look to me to guide you to books and articles, to lectures and courses that will dispel your doubts. Sharing doubts with wise people may also allay them. I will ask God to send the right spiritual companions to you. It will give me great pleasure to see you deepen your knowledge about our heavenly Father and my son.

If you had no doubts, if you understood all mysteries, there would be no room for faith! Stay close to me and you will never lose your faith. I promise.

  ℘ *What about our faith do you find hard to accept? Talk to Mary about it.*

Sleeplessness

April 11

My child, on some nights sleep eludes you, leaving you groggy and unrested in the morning. Perhaps you tussle with issues facing you. Pry those problems from your mind and cast them into my capable hands. I will ask our Lord to solve them for you. Maybe anger or guilt robs you of sleep. Does a physical ache or pain keep you awake? I'd like to siphon it off from you or take it on myself instead. Sometimes you can't pinpoint why you can't sleep. Your mind goes around in circles, replaying the day's events and thinking about what you will do the next day. After trying every suggested remedy, you still lie awake as the night hours creep by. I wish I could sing you a lullaby to ease you into dreamland the way I used to do for Jesus.

I propose a solution you may not have thought of: Pray a rosary. Repeating the rhythmic prayers is soothing and hypnotic. It might lull you to sleep. I like the idea of you falling asleep with me on your mind. As you pray the Hail Marys, you might imagine me holding you close to my heart and rocking you to sleep.

ᘓ *Talk to Mary about any problems you might have sleeping.*

The Present Moment

April 12

My child, time is a mystery we conceive of as past, present, and future. Often your mind dwells in the past, which is gone and unchangeable. Or your mind thinks about the future, which doesn't exist. Because right now is the only real time, I wish you would make the most of it. Be open to the grace God is giving you now.

Ask me to help you to be mindful of your life right now. Stop a moment. For a while forget the past and quit planning for the future. Savor the gift of the present moment. Appreciate that you are alive. Breathe. Feel your heart beating. Look at the world around you carefully with fresh eyes. What new thing do you notice? Realize that I am with you in this present time, loving you.

I thank God with you for the gift of this moment. I pray that you pause like this occasionally because people who do so are happier. And, my dear, I desire your happiness during your life in this slice of time, which is part of an eternity that promises unending happiness.

ᚈ *Relax in the present moment for a while. Then tell Mary what the experience was like for you.*

Laughter

April 13

My child, I love to hear you laugh, for it means you are happy. Some people equate holiness with solemnity, even grimness. It's quite the opposite. Holy people laugh and make others laugh. Baby Jesus often squealed with laughter, delighting Joseph and me. Sometimes all three of us laughed to the point of tears. And some remarks Jesus made while he was teaching were comical. A few of these pertain to our culture, and so you don't realize how humorous they are.

When you carry the weight of the world on your shoulders, you don't feel like laughing. You sigh and plod through the day with your head bent down. Remember that I am here for you. I invite you to shift your burden onto me. Your sadness saddens me. I will be happy to relieve you. Then you will walk with a smile on your face and ready to burst out laughing for the slightest reason. You will laugh at the future, fearless for whatever it holds, and you will laugh at yourself. I, dear child, will laugh with you and look forward to the time when we will be together in heaven, where the halls ring with laughter.

ℭ *When was the last time you had a really good laugh? Ask Mary to help you to see the lighter side of life.*

Catastrophes

April 14

My child, terrible things happen. Natural disasters ravage the earth, and nations war against each other. Personal calamities — a chronic illness, death of a loved one, a divorce — also disrupt and threaten lives. If you are caught in one of these tragedies, how can you weather the storm unscathed? Grab hold of my hand and don't let go!

The challenge you endure may be of such immense proportions that you are tempted to despair. I will entreat the Father on your behalf, asking for the graces of courage and stamina. Then nothing will be too much for you to bear. You will be infused with a moral strength that surprises you. I, who stood at the foot of the cross, will also stand with you.

Have faith in God and in me. We love you and have your welfare at heart. Let me dry your tears and enfold you tenderly in my mantle. Listen to the beating of my immaculate heart. It's brimming with love and sympathy for you. Face the future with hope, dear child, confident that sunnier days are right around the corner.

ᘒ *Speak to Mary about anything that is threatening you now.*

Commercialism

April 15

My child, you are bombarded with voices pressuring you to purchase things. Stores tempt you with reduced prices and special deals. If you seek lasting happiness, accumulating more and more stuff is not the answer. How many tunics, pairs of sandals, and pots do you think I owned? Just what I needed, and it was enough. I had more important things to do than shopping and taking care of a mountain of material things. So do you.

Tune out those voices clamoring for your attention and aiming to sell you something. Resist being a hoarder. Look over your belongings and see what you really do not need. I will be at your side, helping you to decide what to keep and what you can do without. Then donate your surplus to my children who have very little. You will make them and me very happy, my dear.

As Jesus promised, when you are poor in spirit, you will be blessed.[17] With a thinner collection of material things to care for, your step will be lighter. You will have more time and energy to devote to spiritual things, which are priceless.

ඣ *Talk to Mary about your desire to live with less.*

---

[17] Matthew 5:3

Mary's Love

April 16

My child, as my son was dying, he bequeathed to me a precious gift: you! Thoughtful of me to the end, Jesus made sure I would be cared for by entrusting me to John. When he called me John's mother, in effect he confirmed that I was your mother. No mother ever loved a child as ardently as I love my Jesus. I love you with that same burning love.

Each day I watch your progress as you journey toward your ultimate destiny. When you meet up with boulders blocking your path, I'm there to help move them. When you come to a raging river that threatens to swallow you, I see that you cross it safely and dryly. I'm near at hand to help you avoid the hazardous cliffs of temptation. I cheer you on when you walk the narrow road of loving service. Every time you act with integrity, my heart swells with pride.

In return, won't you regard me as your mother? Love me, honor me, and turn to me when you are in need. You won't ever regret it.

ᴄ꙰ *Assure Mary of your love for her and your gratitude for her motherly care.*

Holy Communion

April 17

My child, I eagerly look forward to each time you receive Communion at Mass for several reasons. One is because at that moment you are totally one with Jesus. No person on earth could possibly be as closely united to you as he is in his gift of the sacred bread and wine.

But do you realize that when you receive Communion, you are also united with me? I am intimately one with my son. Where he is, I am. In fact, the body and blood of Jesus that you receive in Communion were formed solely from my flesh and blood. There is another explanation for my being with you in Communion. In the Eucharist you are joined to all of the members of Christ's body. Because I belong to this mystical body and am its mother, it follows that you are united to me.

I long for you to receive Communion as often as you can. On the days you do, the gap between us becomes much narrower. Besides, the grace you receive from my son in those moments of union makes it more likely that someday you and I, child, will be enjoying each other's company at heaven's banquet.

ೞ *Ask Mary to help you to prepare well for receiving Communion and to make a fervent thanksgiving afterward.*

God as Coworker

April 18

My child, you yearn to be successful in all of your undertakings. No one likes the bitter taste of failure. My maternal wish for you is that you experience success in your work and attain your goals, for this brings satisfaction and joy. Scripture warns, "Unless the Lord builds the house, those who build it labor in vain."[18] Today I echo those words to you.

Tackle your work with confidence and zest, but don't assume that you can do it all by yourself. I wouldn't want you to be marred by pride and ambition. The secret to success is to rely on God to help you carry out your work and to bless it. Offer your labor to God and tell him that it is all for his greater glory.

Count on me too as your devoted partner in achieving your goals. I can pray to God for you and give you a little push when you need motivation. I was God's collaborator in the great work of the world's redemption. I can certainly give you a hand as you work out your salvation.

ଔ *Talk to Mary about a project in which you are presently engaged.*

---

[18] Psalm 127:1

Meekness

April 19

My child, Jesus called the meek blessed, so, of course, meekness is a virtue I'd like you to cultivate. Maybe you think meek is synonymous with mousy and weak. On the contrary, it takes strength and self-control to be meek. Meek people are not haughty, stubborn, or self-centered. They do not insist on having their own way. When someone offends them, they do not retaliate.

As the mother of God, I could have insisted on better accommodations in Bethlehem. I could have demanded the choicest vegetables in the market. As Jesus taught crowds, I could have pushed my way to the front to hear him. But with God's grace I didn't.

The meek can accomplish miracles. Moses was the meekest man on earth,[19] but he saved an entire people from slavery. Jesus too was meek, but he saved the world. It is difficult to be meek. When you have the urge to put yourself forward, to seek attention, to force your opinion on others, or to explode when someone offends you, appeal to me for assistance. I will pray that you will have the courage to act like my meek and gentle son and me.

଼ଷ *Talk to Mary about your desire to keep your ego in check.*

---

[19] Numbers 12:3

121

Discouragement

April 20

My child, you don't always reach the bar you set for yourself, and discouragement overshadows you. You break resolutions to diet, exercise, or curb your anger. You pour blood, sweat, and tears into a project only to do something foolish that ruins it. You fall into the same sins over and over. You decide you don't like yourself. If your dissatisfaction is extreme, you might wish you had never been born.

When you are in the dumps like this, don't wallow in self-pity. Let me walk you to a mirror. Look at yourself with me. I see an imperfect person who lives in a broken world. I see someone full of life and potential who dreams big dreams and has setbacks. I see you as one of God's masterpieces, a beloved child of his who is gifted with grace. Most of all, I see someone who means the world to me.

Come, take hold of my arm so I can help you climb out of the pit. I will bring you into a lush meadow where there are blue skies and sunshine. By accepting yourself, flaws and all, you will be at peace and stride confidently into a promising future.

ભ *Tell Mary how grateful you are that she is always there for you, the good mother that she is.*

Praising God

April 21

My child, at certain times, you are moved to praise God. Maybe something fantastic happens — your prayer is answered, you win a prize, or a long lost relative reconnects with you. Perhaps you behold an exceptionally wonderful piece of God's creation. Your spontaneous reaction is to acknowledge the good and provident God who arranged it. That is what I did the day I crossed the threshold of Elizabeth's house. I was so overcome knowing that I carried the Savior within me that I burst out saying, "My soul magnifies the Lord."[20]

Imagine what heaven is like. Millions upon millions of angels and all of us saints are gathered together praising God. When you arrive there, you will realize the countless blessings God rained down on you during your life on earth. You will also behold God in all his glory and beauty and join us in adoration. This is why you were born. As you make your way to your sublime destiny, I walk beside you as a guide. You are never out of my sight. Whenever you praise God in word or song, I add my voice to yours and anticipate doing this with you for all eternity.

ଐ *Review with Mary some of your reasons for praising God.*

---

[20] Luke 1:46

123

Worries

April 22

My child, do thoughts of what might happen weigh heavily on your mind? You may be worrying about your future or what is in store for your loved ones or your country. Your creative mind can conjure up all kinds of alarming happenings. Rest assured, most of them will not come to pass. The time and energy you dedicate to worrying is wasted.

I don't deny that some frightful things lie lurking on your path. Some of them you haven't even imagined. There is no need, however, to be riddled with anxiety. Know that I will face them with you. Trust in me to shield you from serious harm. I will never abandon you. Also believe that God has enormous love for you and will not test you beyond your strength.

So let me scrub those pesky worries from your mind. Do not entertain them and feed them. Instead, picture yourself floating on a limpid pool of water with my loving arms bearing you up. You are relaxed and happy without a care in the world.

That is how your heavenly Father and I would like you to be.

ᘓ *Tell Mary about any worries disturbing your peace today.*

Receiving Compliments

April 22

My child, when someone compliments you for a quality you have, your appearance, or a job well done, accept it graciously. A smile and a simple thank you will do. You might tend to reply in a way that diminishes the kind gesture. For example, if someone remarks that they like your shirt, you might respond, "This old thing? I've had it for years." If someone comments, "That is a neat paint job," you might reply, "Not really. I missed a few spots." Avoid rejecting a compliment in whole or in part.

When Elizabeth greeted me, "Blessed are you among women," I didn't respond, "Not really." Accepting a compliment is an act of love. So is giving a compliment. I like to hear you compliment me in prayers and hymns. I wish you could hear me praising you when you go out of your way to help someone or overcome a temptation. Every day I observe you following in my footsteps even when it's difficult, and I am so proud of you. Perhaps you don't realize the many good qualities you have. I do.

ଓ *Which of Mary's virtues do you particularly admire? Tell her and ask her to help you grow in them.*

Dryness in Prayer

April 23

My child, usually when you pray, you may sense that God and I are very near and loving you. That is a warm, comforting feeling. However, for long or short periods, you may not experience our presence. You might think that we have abandoned you. This dryness in prayer is like standing on the edge of a precipice. It is frightening. You might wonder if you did something wrong or if we are angry with you. In the worst case scenario, you might assume that we are only an illusion.

When you undergo this trial in your prayer life, do not despair. You are in good company — great saints experienced it. Even Jesus cried out from the cross, "My God, my God, why have you forsaken me?"[21] Dryness in prayer is a stage in spiritual growth. Do not stop praying because of it. Varying your method of praying might help.

If the darkness persists, know that I encircle you with my compassionate arms. I will pray for you, my dear, that you emerge from the ordeal stronger and holier. Remember that the ultimate aim of prayer is not the consolations of God but the God of consolation.

ᘓ *Talk to Mary about any trouble you have praying.*

---

[21] Mark 15:34

Bad Days

April 24

My child, no life is free from problems. Some days everything goes wrong for you. You break a dish, you stub your toe, someone scolds you, the milk has turned sour, and to top it off, you are coming down with a cold. You feel like screaming, tearing out your hair, or just sitting down and having a good cry. I sympathize with you in your pain and frustration, although I believe that somewhere in your trials there may be hidden blessings.

In your distress, call out to me with confidence. Address me not as mother but as mamma. I prefer mamma because it is more intimate and more endearing. It is also much more fitting for the close relationship we enjoy. I, your loving mamma, will steer you through those horrible stormy days to the happy sunlit days that surely lie ahead. I will tenderly caress you and calm your frazzled nerves. I'll help you see things in perspective, and new energy will flow into you. Then hand in hand we will take one step at a time together until your problems are nothing but a bad memory.

❧ *Tell Mary how much she means to you.*

Metanoia

April 25

My child, metanoia, or change, is always possible while you are on the face of the earth. You form yourself much as a sculptor models clay. If you are wise, you will make yourself resemble me. Do you have rough edges — such as petty grievances or a quick temper? Smooth them down with a file. Are there weak places, such as a lukewarm faith and lack of courage? Firm these up by adding clay. Are there the unsightly bulges of vices? Remove these and discard them.

If your clay model is a total disaster in your eyes, you can always reduce it to a ball and begin again. In the final stage, you add refinements, delicately shaping the details. You improve your life by growing in virtue.

During all of these steps, I will be a fellow artisan, inspiring you with ideas and steadying and guiding your hand. I will also accompany you into purifying fire that completes and strengthens you. When your earthly task is finished, if it is successful, you will be the person God created you to be. You will come home with me.

℞ *Talk to Mary about changes you think you need to make in yourself in order to become a beautiful person.*

The Mary Way
Our Lady of Good Counsel

April 26

My child, you make decisions every day and all day long: what to wear, what to eat, and what to buy. Once in a while you must make a major decision that impacts your life and that of others, such as where to live, what career to embrace, and whether to marry and if so, whom. When you are not sure what to do, you gather information and consult family members and good friends. Don't forget to also turn to me, your heavenly mother, and let me be your counselor. After all, my Jesus depended on me almost all his life. So can you.

From my vantage point in heaven and as spouse of the Holy Spirit, I'm able to dispense good advice and will gladly whisper it to your heart. When you are confused and in turmoil about a decision, ask my help. I will entreat the Holy Spirit to enlighten you and infuse you with the grace to follow through. I'm eager to put an end to your dilemma so you can be at peace, my child. Of course, my best counsel to you is "do whatever he tells you," he, meaning my son, the Wonder-Counselor.

ɔ *Talk to Mary about a decision you now face.*

Betrayals

April 27

My child, in the course of your life you will find that a few people you thought were your friends do you harm. They may cheat you, tell lies about you, or disappear when you need help. Their betrayal hurts you to the core. Jesus called Judas Iscariot his friend. He had handpicked this apostle, trained him for months, and even trusted him with the group's finances. Imagine how Jesus felt when Judas sold him to his enemies, a move that led to my son's cruel death.

When a friend wounds you, my heart bleeds for you as it did for Jesus. I draw you near, wrap my compassionate arms around you, and hug away your pain. I pray that the bad experience does not prevent you from trusting other friends and making new ones. I pray too that you will find it in your heart to forgive your betrayer.

May you always be a staunch friend to others. I promise to be your everlasting and faithful friend who wants only the best for you. You can place absolute trust in me, my dear.

ഇ *Confide in Mary any sorrow you have resulting from a friend's betrayal.*

Appearances

April 28

My child, your heavenly Father made you just the way you are. I hope you are not dissatisfied with your appearance. Some people think they are too tall or too short. They don't like their pug nose, their stubby fingers, or their freckles. They wish they were as gorgeous or as handsome as models. People who have been disfigured by an accident or disease tend to be embarrassed about the way they look. Fortunate are those who realize that a beautiful soul is far more important than a beautiful body.

I personally love the way you are put together. I wouldn't change a thing. Every aspect of you is beautiful to me, my dear child. What you see as a flaw, I consider charming because it makes you, you, someone who is very precious to me.

When I look at you, it's like looking at a prism through which the light and love and life of God shine through. I pray that like me you look at all of your brothers and sisters — no matter what size, shape, or color — with eyes of love.

cs *Talk with Mary about how you use your body to give glory to God.*

Exhausted?

April 29

My child, some days you are so tired that moving your little finger seems an exertion beyond you. You can't think straight. You long to fall on your bed and sleep for twenty-four hours. You were busy carrying out umpteen chores, meeting responsibilities, answering requests, and coping with unexpected jobs. Now you are so fatigued that you feel as though all the air has been sucked out of you. There were days when I felt the same, especially when Nazareth was buffeted by sandstorms or incredibly hot so that sweat trickled down my back.

My poor child, in case no one else thanks you, I thank you for pouring yourself out for others! Now that you are drained, relax and put your feet up. Have no regrets about tasks you didn't get around to. Don't think about the workload that awaits you tomorrow. Just savor a pause in your hectic life and let me massage the knotted muscles in your neck and back. Soon you will rise with renewed energy, ready to tackle the next project. Turn all your efforts into gold by offering them through my hands to God. They will culminate in eternal rest.

ख *Talk to Mary about your fatigue. Ask her to pray that your strength be renewed.*

Pleasing People

April 30

My child, as a social being, you like to please others. You want people to think well of you and accept you. Pleasing people could be either good or bad. In general, doing as others wish makes them happy and therefore shows love. If, however, people expect you to do something wrong, do not comply even though you risk angering or alienating them. Yes, you might lose a friend, your reputation, or your job. But refusing to sin shows love for yourself. It increases your chance of capturing the valuable prize at the end of your race.

If you are the victim of waves of negative peer pressure, pray to me for courage and strength to stand firmly against them. I will defend you like a shield protecting your precious soul. Keep in mind that the One you are obliged to please over everyone else is God. You accomplish this by listening to your heavenly Father and carrying out his will.

Do you know what pleases me, your loving mother, most? When you act as a true child of God and my beloved child. Then a brilliant smile crosses my face.

℘ *Is someone pressuring you to do wrong? Talk to Mary about it and ask her help.*

May

A Marian Month

May 1

My child, you remember me in a special way during May. This is the month I would have chosen too because in May the world awakens from the dead of winter and spring is at its peak. Let the multicolored flowers beautifying gardens and the rich green carpets of grass remind you of the new creation brought about by my son. Also, let your mind turn to me, his mother, who enabled the rebirth of the world.

When you honor me by placing flowers before my image, by crowning it, by planting a Mary garden, and by praying extra prayers to me, I am deeply touched, dear. These acts declare your love for me in an unmistakable way. I treasure every one of them as though it were a precious jewel. In return, I promise to always be mother to you—cherishing you, protecting you, and guiding you as you live through each day. My heart's desire is that I lead you directly to my son, who loves you with an infinite love, as his death proved. Only when you follow him unreservedly will I be satisfied. That is the most excellent gift you can give me—like pure gold.

cg *Tell Mary of your deep love for her and gratitude to her.*

Loved Ones

May 2

My child, your life is intimately intertwined with the lives of your family members and friends. It is almost as though they are part of you. When they are happy and their lives are going smoothly, you are happy. But when they are suffering or in harm's way, you suffer. No son loved a mother as much as Jesus loved me. One searing pain he endured on the cross was knowing that his death caused me great anguish.

When loved ones are in physical or moral danger, you would go to the ends of the earth to save them. You give them advice, consult others, devote time and perhaps your money to rescue them out of their black hole. The surest way you can help them, is by putting them into my compassionate hands.

You may care deeply for your loved ones, but your heavenly Father and I love them even more. Besides, the love I have for you is as fathomless as the ocean. So do pray to me for your loved ones who are in peril, and I will do everything in my power to restore joy to their hearts and yours.

ଭ *Talk to Mary about a loved one you are concerned about.*

Remorse

May 3

My child, so far your journey to heaven hasn't always followed a direct route. You made wrong turns and zigzagged. Sometimes you headed in the totally opposite direction! You regret these lapses and are ashamed of them. They torment you even though you have been forgiven. I assure you that I have forgotten them, and you too should blot them out of your mind. The precious blood of my son effectively washed away all of your sins and offenses. You, my dear, have nothing to worry about.

Jesus taught that the Father is as thrilled when a backslider repents as a woman who finds a lost coin, a shepherd who recovers a lost sheep, and a father whose wayward son returns home. The Father's willingness to forgive was a lesson my son couldn't repeat often enough. Believe him. In the future, when you depart from the right way, depend on me to call you back to it. Arm and arm we will walk straight toward God, who is waiting at heaven's gates with infinite love in his eyes. He and I desire only your happiness—pure, unadulterated joy.

ଔ *Does a particular past failing continue to spoil your joy? Tell Mary about it.*

Change of Plans

May 4

My child, you may pride yourself on planning your life to the last detail—not only where you will live, your occupation, and who you will share your life with, but how your day will unfold tomorrow. As you know, God sometimes has other plans for you that supersede yours. Don't let that rattle you or shake your faith. Trust that God in his wisdom and love is working out a superb pattern for your life that ultimately is the best for you. It is tailored to fit you perfectly.

To you, the divine plan may appear flawed, if not disastrous. You may want to protest and demand a change to align it more with your hopes and dreams. Look to me to help you deal with the mystifying inevitable. I fully understand your frustration, dear, and my motherly heart longs to comfort and soothe you. Together let's step bravely into the future that is shrouded in uncertainty. God's ways are truly mystifying, but eventually all may become clear to you, if not in this world, in the next. That's been my experience.

ଓ *Speak to Mary about a time when God's plans replaced yours to your dismay.*

Courage
Queen of Apostles

May 5
Saturday after Ascension

My child, at times you must summon up great courage to be true to God and especially to spread your faith to others. After the Ascension, the apostles were befuddled and hesitant about obeying Jesus' command to go out to make disciples of all nations.[22] I prayed with them in the upper room, asking God to come and strengthen them. After the Holy Spirit descended on them, I continued to inspire and encourage them. And that, my child, is what I do for you.

I pray that you may be a good apostle, filled with zeal for bringing other people to my son. He and I depend on you for that. Don't be shy when it comes to speaking about your belief in Jesus. Show your faith by something as simple as praying grace before meals wherever you are.

Is being an active apostle something new and uncomfortable? I will help you take baby steps in this venture. You may not be a priest, deacon, or catechist, but neither was I. Sometimes the most persuasive strategy in drawing people to the faith is by living it.

℞ *Tell Mary how you were an apostle and ways you could be.*

---

[22] Matthew 28:19

Channel of Grace
Mediatrix of All Graces

May 6

My child, every good that God bestows on you and his very life in you comes through me. Because I cooperated with God's outrageous plan two thousand years ago, salvation was made possible through my son's death and resurrection. Ever since then, day after day your heavenly Father sends graces flowing to earth through my maternal hands. An enormous store of them is available, which I am eager to dispense to you. Never hesitate to implore me for graces. They are yours for the asking.

What grace do you wish you had today? Is it the grace to be patient, to grow in faith, to be more loving, to carry out your job, to bear suffering, to pray better, to break free from the clutches of an addiction, to fulfill your responsibilities? Just name it, and I will gladly ask my son to send that grace to you, for I am your mother who loves you. Being mother to Jesus and to you is what I was born for. Do people you know need a particular grace? Be a channel yourself by recommending them to me. I will take care of them too out of love for you and them.

❧ Talk to Mary about a grace you or someone you know is in need of today.

139

Mary Garden

May 7

My child, don't you agree that flowers are one of God's loveliest creations? Even flowers that are considered weeds have a certain beauty. I enjoyed watching the flowers around our house bloom each year. As a child, Jesus would present me with flowers he picked, and their fragrance filled our house. Later, he described the lilies of the field as being clothed more gloriously than Solomon. Knowing that Jesus also appreciated flowers made me happy. It also makes me happy when you place a vase of flowers before my image or when you crown me with a floral wreath.

Many flowers are associated with me. Some bear my name, such as marigold and rosemary. Others are compared to my qualities or my things. For example, violets stand for my innocence, lilies of the valley for my tears, and morning glories for my mantle. Legends have sprung up about the role of flowers in my life.

You might plant a Mary garden with flowers related to me as some parishes do. It will remind you to think of me. I would like that.

ᘓ *Find out about flowers related to Mary and talk to her about them.*

Letting Go

May 8

My child, your life rolls along merrily until something you value is taken from you. You lose a favorite book, your job, or a pet. A fire destroys your possessions, or robbers steal them. You might have to move from your comfortable home, or someone close to you may die. As years pass, your health and good looks diminish. Losses like these throw you off-kilter and frustrate you. Naturally you are disappointed and sad. I am familiar with losing things and people I love.

You can react to losses in different ways. You can be angry and become bitter. I wouldn't want you to feel this way because you harm yourself and make life unpleasant for others. The alternative is to gracefully accept unwelcome changes as a fact of life and trust that they are in keeping with God's ineffable plan for you.

Pour out your distress to me, my child. I will wrap you in my loving arms. I will pray that you have the grace to let go and walk bravely into the future with me at your side, expecting new gifts that you haven't even imagined.

ରେ *What are you finding hard to let go? Tell Mary about it.*

Making God's Love Visible

May 9

My dear, God has a vast love for human beings, and he looks to you to reveal it to them. I revealed it by bringing Love incarnate into the world. Now I will help you to make it visible and palpable. Let God's love shine in your eyes by gazing on others with concern and encouragement. Let it radiate from your smile, giving comfort and joy to people. Let God's love flow from your hands as your serve your family and minister to those who are in need. Let God's love be evident as your feet take you to marches for peace and justice or to funeral parlors to comfort the bereaved.

Your whole being is a vessel of God, for he lives within you. Unleash his awesome love by your words and actions. Do you doubt that you can do this task that is tantamount to being like God? I acknowledge that you are a broken vessel. Still, in his goodness God has provided me as your mother and aide. I will nurture the God-life in you so that people with whom you come in contact will know their heavenly Father and love him in return.

ଓ *Tell Mary what Godlike things you are planning today.*

Procrastination

May 10

My child, how easily you fall into the trap of putting off things, particularly if they are disagreeable. Watch out! Procrastination could be a symptom of laziness or sloth. You might delay scheduling needed doctor appointments; visiting a lonely, grumpy relative; or going on a diet. You just might not feel like fixing the door that's been broken for weeks or cleaning the messy stove. You might be postponing spiritual tasks, too, such as going to confession. The longer you wait to spring into action, the longer the task weighs on your mind. You drag from one day to the next with a niggling guilt you try to ignore.

I want you to be totally free from problems, even the slightest ones, so you thoroughly enjoy being alive. For that reason, I invite you to ask me to obtain for you the motivation and the ambition to tackle certain deferred tasks as well as the energy to complete them. Imagine how relieved you will be once they are completed. And I will be very happy for you, dear.

ca *Are there tasks you have been postponing? Ask Mary to help you to get busy so you can cross them off your to do list.*

Be Positive!

May 11

My child, people who have a positive outlook on life are considerably happier than those who do not. I'd like you to be a lighthearted person who is a delight to be with, not a depressing sourpuss. So let me coach you on ways to be positive. When bad things occur, search for some good aspect or result. Even the tragic original sin became a happy fault because it led to stupendous graces for the human race.

View people with an eye for their good features. The most dastardly persons and those who have wronged you have some redeeming qualities, though you may have to squint to detect them. Jesus could have given up on Peter for his impulsiveness and disloyalty, but instead he made him leader of the early Church.

Lastly, look to the future with hope in your heart. If an event can turn out to be good or bad, count on it to be good. Each day as you arise, say to yourself, "This is going to be a great day." Then chances are it will be, especially if you keep your heart connected to mine.

ᚲᛉ *Do you tend to see a glass as half empty or half full? Talk over your attitudes with Mary.*

Our Daily Bread
Our Lady of the Blessed Sacrament

May 12
The eve of this feast

My child, I prepared bread for my family daily. During the thirty years Jesus lived with me, he often saw me grind grain, knead dough, and bake bread. It could be that watching me one day, Jesus was inspired to remain with you on earth in the form of bread. To be food that people would eat was an incredible idea. It was also ingenious because bread is a basic food. It is easily made and found on tables all over the world.

The God-man who took his flesh and blood from me now makes his flesh and blood available every day for his followers to consume in the forms of bread and wine. That intimate communion has no parallel. No one can come closer to you than Jesus does.

My hope is that you take advantage of this miracle often. Doing so will draw you more deeply into a relationship with Jesus and also with me. I encourage you, too, to visit Jesus living in tabernacles as sacred bread. While you are in the church or chapel, remember to stop by my statue or picture and say hello to me.

ᴓ *Talk to Mary about her son's amazing gift of himself in the Eucharist.*

Mary's Visits
Our Lady of Fatima

May 13

My child, since my assumption, I visited earth a number of times. I appeared to people of all ages, saints and sinners, and often to children. Some apparitions you are acquainted with, such as at Lourdes and Fatima. Others no one knows about except the visionaries.

I realize that sometimes you must wish that you, too, could see me in person. After all, it's rather difficult to converse with someone who is invisible. Sometimes you might even doubt that I exist. As for most people, however, you must wait until you enter the next world to see me. Then you will behold the love I have for you written on my face, and you will feel my arms wrapping you in a warm embrace of welcome.

In the meantime, be convinced that I am real and I do hear your prayers (even those you say half-heartedly or as though in a stupor). Be consoled by remembering that Jesus declared, "Blessed are those who have not seen and yet have come to believe."[23] He referred to himself, but his words also hold true regarding me, your loving mother.

℞ *Tell Mary how you long to meet her face-to-face one day.*

---

[23] John 20:29

Dancing for the Lord

May 14

My child, some religions banned dancing, but it has a long tradition in our faith. Miriam, the sister of Moses, led the women in dancing to celebrate the escape from Egypt. King David danced before the Ark of the Covenant. At the wedding feast in Cana, I danced with the women, and Jesus danced with the men. Dancing is a wonderful expression of joy.

Dancing as prayer can be a beautiful thing. When you dance, you use your whole body and expend a great deal of energy, far more than when you say or sing prayer. Dancing is a wonderful way to glorify God. Scripture exhorts, "Let them praise his name with dancing, making melody to him with tambourine and lyre."[24]

You might have a chance to incorporate dance into a prayer service. If you are not comfortable dancing before others, you can still dance as prayer in the privacy of your home. I will be delighted to see you worshiping God this way. You may be an accomplished dancer, but even if you are awkward and clumsy, I will be glad to offer your dance to our Lord. No doubt, it will make him smile.

ଓ *Talk to Mary about ways you might pray through dancing.*

---

[24] Psalm 149:3

Consolation
Comforter of the Afflicted

May 15

My child, when faced either with a crisis like a flood that destroys your home or with a constant irritation like a rude neighbor or a jealous enemy, I am there for you. Someone who has suffered has excellent empathy for another sufferer. You are aware of the hardships I endured, culminating in the terrible death of my son. Surely then I can identify with you as you are enmeshed in suffering no matter how extreme. Besides that, I am your heavenly mother, and who is a better consoler than a mother? You can never fathom the depth and breadth of my love for you.

So, darling, flee to me at the first sign of trouble. Don't wait until you are absolutely miserable. I will do all in my power to relieve your distress. I will ask Jesus to spare you or else to give you the strength to endure whatever trial you are going through. I will enfold you in my arms and soothe you until the storm has past and the sun's golden rays shine on you once more.

෬ *Are you in the grip of a crisis? If so, ask Mary for help. If not, tell her you are confident she will always rescue you.*

Life to the Fullest

May 16

My child, you might feel sometimes that days drag. I assure you, though, that life is short. As Scripture says, "The days of our life are seventy years, or perhaps eighty, if we are strong."[25] From my perspective now — two thousand years after I lived in Galilee — seventy years is just a hiccup in the span of time. Your life on earth will pass quickly, so make the most of it.

Soak in the beauty of the world, the seasons, the animals and flowers. Use your gifts and powers to the utmost and enjoy them. Savor the love others have for you and be generous in bestowing yours. Above all, don't neglect your spiritual life. Grow strong in virtue and cultivate your friendship with God and with me. There will be distractions; but if you ask me, I will help you stay focused on what really matters in life. I hope with all my heart that when you reach the end of your earthly days, you will be with me, your loving mother, and Jesus, who called himself the way, the truth and the life.[26]

ॐ *Talk to Mary about your desire to live life to the hilt.*

---

[25] Psalm 90:10

[26] John 14:6

Thwarted

May 17

My child, today you may be striving to attain a goal you have your heart set on. However, you might encounter a brick wall. People or circumstances can halt your progress and put a damper on your ambition. Of course, at first you will be deflated. Shake off your feelings of discouragement. If your goal is a worthy one, don't give up! Throw your knapsack over the wall and count on reaching your goal. It will not be impossible if you enlist my assistance. I will ask my son to break down the wall so your dreams will not be doomed.

Be patient, though. It might take a while to clear the way before you. It may be that you will need to take another route that goes around that wall. Listen to the Holy Spirit whispering in your heart. He may suggest another course of action. Be open to whatever God wills for you because he only wants what is best for you, as I do. In any case, I will be walking with you. Lean on me for support whenever you need to. I'm always ready to help you, dear.

ɔঽ *What are you aiming for today? Ask Mary for assistance.*

Simplicity

May 18

My child, Jesus taught, "Whoever does not receive the kingdom of God as a little child will never enter it."[27] One childlike quality that I recommend to you is simplicity. A child's life is not complicated by a mountain of possessions and a compulsion to increase it. A child derives pleasure from simple things like watching an ant or jumping into a pile of leaves. A child doesn't make convoluted plans for the future but is totally absorbed in the present moment. My son is a model of simplicity. He could have chosen to appear on earth with all the trappings of a noble in some grand kingdom. Instead he came as a carpenter in an obscure village.

I definitely hope that you will join me in God's kingdom someday. What extra baggage slows you down on your way there? Maybe it's time to rid yourself of clutter by giving it away. Can you simplify your life by streamlining your calendar? Then you would have more time to enjoy the present moment and wonder at God's gifts. Becoming simple may intimidate you, but I will give you a hand if you let me.

Ask Mary to help you divest yourself of anything that prevents you from having a childlike simplicity.

---

[27] Luke 18:17

Thirsting for God

May 19

My child, I read your heart and know that you long for love, happiness, and meaning in your life. Those longings are only satisfied by possessing God. It is God you actually desire. You can identify with the psalmist who prayed, "My soul thirsts for God, for the living God."[28] The holy One who created you out of love, longs for you too, even more than you long for him. I am dedicated to two things: pleasing God and making you happy, my dear child.

Through my prayers for you, your faith will grow stronger each day. When it falters, I will swiftly implore God for grace for you. As you go through your day, if you depart from the safe path to heaven, I will be with you to gently guide you back. I will be at your side to nudge you to do the loving things that God expects from you. Jesus and I are never separated. Our unconditional love for you will see that you reach the eternal shore where your Father is waiting for you at the end of your journey. At last you will be one with God. Your thirst will be quenched.

 times *Tell Mary how much you yearn for God.*

---

[28] Psalm 42:22

Surrender

May 20

My child, at times things do not go the way you think is best. You run into bumps in the road that test your patience. Try not to rant and rave, which only increases your aggravation and upsets others. Rather, surrender quietly to the inevitable as part of God's mysterious plan and accept such trials as calmly and as unsinkable as a cork floating on a river. Trust that no matter what the problems are, I am always with you and supporting you as your devoted mother. With my help and God's grace eventually you will triumph.

In the meantime, if you feel beaten and bruised, lean back into my loving arms. I will console you and restore your serenity. Hear me remind you that your troubles will not last forever. They will pass and fade. The way before you will be smooth and straight once again. Also, you, my dear, will be stronger for having ploughed through the difficulties instead of running away from them or fighting them. Other people will look to you as a light as they travel along their own paths.

☙ *What problems are you dealing with at the present time? Take them to Mary.*

In Time of Need

May 21

My child, I love you from the bottom of my heart and would do anything to please you and bring you joy. When you are in need of something for yourself or for someone else, you do not have to rely solely on yourself. Request my help. I will be touched by your confidence in me and will take your prayer to my son. Do not be surprised if he answers, "No" or "Wait a little longer." In his wisdom, Jesus will respond in the way that is best for you and others. Leave the outcome up to him.

If your request is denied, you will not understand and will enter the zone of mystery. Do not let this harden your heart toward God or let it make you doubt his immense love for you. I assure you that in the end all will be well. Come to me and bury your disappointment in my heart. I will ease your pain. I too sometimes failed to understand God's mysterious ways, but I always knew his goodness was beyond measure. You can trust him with all your being as I did, dear.

ભ *Do you have a special prayer intention today? Place it in Mary's hands.*

The Invisible World

May 22

My child, some things are impossible to perceive with your senses, for instance, your own soul. You can't see thoughts or love, but they are real. The whole supernatural world is also an unseen reality. You are surrounded by invisible angels, including your guardian angel. You have never seen God, but I assure you, God exists and is ever present to you. I too am your hidden companion, your loving mother who lingers on earth to care for you.

If you wish to be more attuned to this unseen world, spend time with us. Occasionally during the course of the day stop your activities, be quiet, and commune with us. I would be delighted if you were more aware of me watching over you and right at your elbow ready to assist you in any way I can. I will help you to be friends with my son, to be on fire with the Spirit's gifts, and to know the tenderness of the Father's love for you. Your belief in the unseen world will deepen. I will be as real to you as the woman who gave you birth.

ଔ *Spend time with Mary simply enjoying her company and telling her whatever is on your mind.*

Safe Travels
Our Lady of the Wayside

May 23
The eve of this feast

My child, Our Lady of the Wayside is a fitting
title for me. I made seven long journeys, which was
unusual for a Jewish woman. Sometimes I followed Jesus.
I traveled either by donkey or walked. Now I am the
patron of travelers. As you take trips, whatever your mode
of transportation, call upon me for protection. I will see
that you are safe from accidents and don't lose your way.

More important, you are a pilgrim on earth on
journey to your eternal home. I will be happy to guide
your steps as you make your way there, following Jesus.
The road may be rough and twisting. Detours may
confuse you. With my help you will skirt treacherous
mountains, locate bridges over raging rivers, and avoid
dangerous chasms. When you stumble and fall, I will be
there to lift you up. When you grow weary, I will ask God
to infuse you with a surge of energy. My dear, at some
points I will even carry you as a mother carries her
beloved child close to her heart. What a joy it will be for
both of us when you reach your destination.

ଓ *Talk to Mary about her journeys and yours.*

Defense Against Enemies
Mary, Help of Christians

May 24

My child, I weep at the ongoing persecution of Christians. During my lifetime, John the Baptist and some of my son's early followers were martyred. James was the first apostle killed for believing in Jesus. Today my children all over the world are suffering from enemies. Pray, and I will come to their defense. I will rally Jesus and legions of angels to protect them. On your part, offer sacrifices and do penance for them.

You, dear child, are the target of supernatural evil forces much stronger than earthly enemies. By cooperating with the Incarnation, I helped Jesus crush Satan and his minions. In Scripture the dragon, a symbol of Satan, makes war on the rest of my children who obey God and witness to Jesus.[29] When you suffer an onslaught of temptations to give up your faith or to veer from following the way of Jesus, call upon me. I am your devoted and strong ally. I will rush to your side, snatch you away from the powers of darkness, and cover you with my protective mantle.

CR *Mention to Mary those Christians who are under attack today and ask for her prayers.*

---

[29] Revelation 12:17

Mary's Son

May 25

My child, as the mother of Jesus, I'm aware of the deep and lasting love he bears toward you. Why else would he stoop to become like one of us limited creatures? Why else would he submit to cruel tortures and an excruciating execution? If you were the only one in the world, Jesus still would have come to earth to save you. My motherly wish is that you respond to his love with your whole heart.

Keep close to my son during the day. He dwells in the depths of your being, so speak to him frequently. Share your joys and sorrows with him. When you dread a challenge that an upcoming day holds, depend on Jesus to be with you, sustaining you with his grace. Receive him often in Communion. Then you will be fortified to meet cheerfully whatever comes your way.

Over and over I implore Jesus to shower down the choicest blessings on you, and he is always glad to comply. In all the ups and downs of your life, the two of us, your loving mother and your divine brother, will be sticking with you whether you sense it or not.

ಏ *Tell Mary how much you would like to become even closer to her son.*

Mysteries

May 26

My child, many things happen in the world and in your life that puzzle you. When you don't understand mysteries such as why good people suffer or why your carefully laid plans did not bear fruit, you are frustrated. You want to rebel against the way things are, but to your dismay, you realize that you are helpless to effect change. You also know that usually no one on earth can explain things to you. That is when your faith has to take over.

I pray for you, dear, that you firmly trust in our good and gracious God. I assure you that our Creator providentially and tenderly arranges every detail of your life. From your viewpoint on earth and with your limited mind, you can't possibly comprehend all the complex workings of God, not even if you pondered them a thousand years. I don't understand everything either.

Relax in the knowledge that God is in control and he loves you. In eternity many of the pieces will fall into place. There you and I will marvel together at the glorious deeds of the Lord, in particular those on your behalf.

ଓ *Share with Mary puzzling things you do not understand that bother you.*

No Comparing!

May 27

My child, people are all different, like the various flowers that make a garden beautiful. The world would be much duller if roses were the only flowers. You might be dissatisfied with yourself when other people excel in some area. You might wish you had their talents, their athletic prowess, their good looks, or their sterling qualities. God doesn't love these people any more than he loves you. He made you unlike anyone else and treasures you as you are. You have your own gifts, and God also gave you a definite purpose in life not assigned to anyone else.

On the other hand, many people are less gifted than you in some regards. Refrain from judging them or looking down on them. Concentrate on developing the facets of your own life that are in your control. I will be with you, encouraging you to be the best person you can be and begging God for the graces that would make you your true self, how he dreamed you would be. Relinquish your tendency to compare yourself with others. Ignore any demeaning comments others make about you. Then you will be much happier and I will be too.

❧ *Talk to Mary about how you could develop one of your gifts.*

Loving Others

May 28

My child, Jesus said that the second greatest commandment is to love your neighbor as yourself.[30] Some people are easy to love, while loving some others is like hugging a porcupine. For me, it was uncomfortable to be in the company of a few neighbors, like the woman who talked nonstop and the man who always found fault with Joseph's work. Nevertheless, I showed them love.

What complicates loving others is your tendency to love yourself more. Are you tempted to use others for your own purposes? Do you pride yourself on being more successful than others, or worse, prevent them from being successful? Do you ignore or badmouth someone for whom you have a natural aversion? When you hurt my other children, you hurt me.

The remedy for too much self-love is to stay close to my son. The more you love him, the easier it is to love others. You will be close to Jesus if you stay close to me. I'm always available. When you are united with Jesus and me, God's love will filter through you to others.

ℭ *Is there someone you find difficult to love? Tell Mary how you would like to love this person and ask her help.*

---

[30] Matthew 22:38–39

161

One Benefit of Tribulations

May 29

My child, naturally you would prefer not to have trials and tribulations spoil your happy life. But they are unavoidable. Did you ever consider that when your days are running along smoothly, you are happy and content but may forget me and Jesus? You fill your hours with dozens of activities, some necessary and some trivial, but perhaps skip prayers, even Mass. That is no way to lead a successful life. It will not end in lasting peace and happiness.

However, when a tragedy breaks into your life or you are entangled in some predicament, ah, in your distress, you turn to me for help. You suddenly restore communication with me and perhaps rope others into praying to me too. I'm glad of that, for I love to help you solve your problems. I love to clasp you to my heart and console you. Because tribulations drive you to me and Jesus, I'm grateful that God plants them along your way every once in a while. They remind you that you have a mother in heaven who cares deeply about you.

ભ *Tell Mary that you do not want to lose sight of her and her son on ordinary days.*

Harmony

May 30

My child, the very fact that you exist endows you with great power. Every kind word you say and every loving deed you do contribute to the total harmony of the universe. Your life is interwoven with the life of everyone who ever lived, lives, or will live. This is a grave responsibility, which you might find overwhelming. But don't be frightened. You are not alone.

Page by page I go through the score of your life with you, asking God to empower you to recognize and perform what is right and good. I assume the role of a conductor who leads you as you play your part in a grand symphony. Listen to me, keep your eyes on me, study my face carefully, and you will not be inclined to play a jarring note. If you faithfully do this, you will be in tune with God's stupendous masterpiece. Then someday I, your loving mother, will proudly usher you in through heaven's gates to join in the chorus of saints and angels who make music for the Lord eternally.

CR *Tell Mary you wish to be as faithful to living according to God's plan as she was.*

Holy Boldness
Visitation of the Blessed Virgin Mary

May 31

My child, loving others can involve bravely taking risks. When I learned that my elderly cousin Elizabeth was six months pregnant, I knew she could use my help. Common sense dictated that a woman carrying the Son of God should take extreme care of herself. But how could I stay safe at home while Elizabeth needed me? So I traveled ninety-some miles to her house under the hot sun and over the rocky and often uphill roads, where bandits might lurk. And I'm glad I did.

Being a Christian requires such holy boldness at times. Dare to do something difficult to show love for God and others. Join a charitable organization, serve meals to the hungry, accompany the dying, shop for a housebound neighbor. The possibilities are endless. Approach the challenging task you choose hand in hand with me, and you will have the fortitude to follow through. Be conscious of my presence as I support you with love and pride. Critics may call you foolish, but you too will be glad you showed holy boldness. So will people who benefit from your courageous action.

ᐸᔿ *Talk to Mary about how you can show holy boldness today. Then take the first step.*

June

The Sacred Heart of Jesus

June 1

My child, the month of June is dedicated to my son's Sacred Heart. Hearts stand for life, our whole being, and love. The heart of Jesus formed in my womb out of my flesh and blood, is a symbol of his immense love for you. The almighty God condescended to become a man. What tremendous love! Every heartbeat of Jesus was a divine act of love. The Sacred Heart is still aflame with burning, passionate love for you.

I'll never forget the day I watched as a soldier thrust his lance into the side of Jesus, piercing his heart. I thought my heart would stop. Jesus offered himself for love of you. His sacrifice on the cross was also my sacrifice: my son for your eternal life. I don't regret it. Because Jesus loves you so much, I also do. I love you with the vast, unconditional love of a mother. Love sometimes hurts. It often calls for sacrifice. Jesus and I yearn for your love in return. Will you give us your heart? Will you live for God with all your heart? Will you be faithful to us until your last heartbeat?

 os *Tell Mary how deeply you love her son.*

Dealing with Failure

June 2

My child, you've learned by now that you do not always achieve success, not even when you try with all of your might. You aim for something but stumble along the way to it, and it eludes you. Perhaps other people block you from reaching your goal or circumstances defeat you. Of course, you are disappointed, but do not be so disheartened by these failures that you lose confidence in yourself and become reluctant to try for anything major again. Rely on me to spur you on to even greater things and to be a firm support to you in accomplishing them.

Failures can be stepping stones to virtues like humility, courage, and perseverance. They might also prompt you to turn to me, your mother who loves you, for aid in setting new goals, striving for them with renewed ambition, and eventually achieving them. Tears and bitterness won't do. Smile bravely, my dear, and plan your strategy for winning the next time you attempt a feat. Don't be afraid to aim high, for with me to uphold you, wonderful goals are within your reach. I promise.

   What are your short-term and long-term goals? Share them with Mary and ask for her help in procuring them.

Alert to Miracles

June 3

My child, when you rise in the morning, thank God for another day of life, another day to love him. Of course, everything won't unfold to your liking. In fact, horrible things might occur to mar your day and drag down your spirits. But trust me, some of the hours before you will hold special gifts, even little miracles. Keep your eyes open and you will see signs of your Father's love for you: the exquisite play of the shadow of leaves on your wall, a friend contacting you out of the blue, the remarkable avoidance of an accident. Events like these are not by chance, mere serendipities. No, they are deliberately and delicately woven into the fabric of your life by the divine hand.

At the very start of the day, make up your mind to be sensitive to all of the presents your heavenly Father will bestow on you. In the course of the day frequently turn to me and ask me to point them out to you. Then each time you realize one of these gifts, join your voice to mine in thanking and praising God.

ℰ *With Mary review the previous day. Talk to her about the miracles you discover in it.*

Precious Tears

June 4

My child, you might regard crying as a curse and an embarrassment. It distorts your face and leaves you with puffy, bloodshot eyes and a red nose. Tears are precious when they are a sign of remorse. Mostly you cry when you are sad. In one of its most tender verses, Scripture says that God collects your tears in a bottle.[31] That is how much he loves you. Shedding tears is nothing to be ashamed of. Jesus cried when his friend Lazarus died, and I wept grievously when Jesus died. When you cry because you are overcome with sorrow for yourself or in sympathy for another person's plight, I long to dry your tears and hold you close to my heart.

Tears flow too when you are moved by an exquisite sight such as the Alps viewed from a plane or the tiny face of a newborn. Also when you are ecstatically happy, you might burst into tears.

Tears may be shed during an intense experience of God. This is called the gift of tears and is a spiritual gift from the Holy Spirit. These are the tears I wish for you.

CR *When have you cried? Talk to Mary about these times.*

---

[31] Psalm 56:8

Seeking God

June 5

My child, you were created to be one with the all-holy God, and you are restless and incomplete until then. How you long for your heavenly Father! On earth you wander about searching for him. You want to feel God's presence and be comforted by the sure knowledge of his love for you. You try to come in touch with God through prayers and religious rituals. You strive to know more about God by reading about him and talking about him to others. But to your dismay sometimes God hides from you, leaving you feeling alone and in the dark. You wonder what is wrong.

Long ago I brought God into the world and gave him a face. I showed him to shepherds and kings, saints and sinners. Take my hand and I will gladly lead you straight to him. I will ask God to make himself known to you in unmistakable ways. God answers my prayers. Be prepared for a divine revelation that will flood your heart with peace and joy. This will only be a taste of the happiness that will be yours when you are united with God in heaven.

CR *Tell Mary of your desire to more deeply know God's presence and love.*

A Hopeful Heart

June 6

My child, at times you may be overwhelmed by the state of the world or by some personal disaster that shakes you to the core. You feel as though you are trapped in a dark dungeon. You are sunk in a mire of sadness and perhaps even on the dangerous brink of despair. That is a lonely and desperate place to be.

When you are devastated by the cruel twists in your life, my heart goes out to you. Cry, "Mother Mary, help me," and I will hasten to you. I will enfold you, stroke your head, and let you nestle in my arms. I will remind you that God promised, "When you pass through the waters, I will be with you; and through the rivers they shall not overwhelm you; when you walk through fire you shall not be burned."[32] You will survive; so keep your chin up, stand tall, and expect the rays of the sun to break through the gloom.

A child of mine can always hope. Trust my love and your heavenly Father's love to be sure protections against any tragedy destroying your positive outlook.

ભ *Tell Mary you are confident that she will be with you during any trials.*

---

[32] Isaiah 43:1–2

Missing Thanks

June 7

My child, are you ever hurt because of someone's lack of gratitude? You might go out of your way to be kind or do a favor, and the person you helped just takes it for granted. He or she doesn't say thank you or express gratitude with a gift. When that happens, you might feel like never doing a good deed for someone again—at least not for that ungrateful person!

Don't let hurt feelings get the best of you. I'm fully aware of all of your kindnesses to others, and I thank you for them. So does my son. If you recall, nine out of ten lepers whom he healed didn't bother to express thanks to him either.[33] But that didn't stop him from doing good.

The lesson to take away from your experience is to remember how bad you felt at not being acknowledged and determine not to make anyone else feel that way. I will prompt you. By the way, when God blesses you in some way, be quick to say thank you to him. And as often as possible participate in Mass, the greatest prayer of thanksgiving. I will be there too.

CR *Thank Mary for what she has done and is doing for you.*

---

[33] Luke 17:11–19

A Wise Teacher
Mary, Seat of Wisdom

June 8

My child, in case this title of mine, Seat of Wisdom, puzzles you, let me explain. I was the site where the Son of God, who is wisdom and truth, grew for nine months. Later, my lap was literally his seat as I fed him, taught him to speak, and put on his little sandals. Another meaning of this title is that I am a wise virgin. I am wise in the ways of the Lord. I know about God, what he does, and what pleases him.

You prize your education through which you plumb the secrets of the secular world. I invite you to sit at my feet and learn from me a far more important and life-giving knowledge. As I taught Jesus, I will teach you how to be the best human being you can be. Study my life and my virtues. Let me steer you away from false teachers whose instruction would lead you astray and ultimately harm you. When you take me as your teacher, you too will become wise. You will see things as God sees them.

cχ *Talk to Mary about what you would like her to teach you.*

Your True Worth

June 9

My child, are you discouraged because you haven't accomplished any major feat? You haven't won any awards, saved anyone's life, or become famous. Your works are not displayed and admired by multitudes. Don't be concerned. I want to impress on you the fact that in my eyes and in God's what you do is not as important as who you are. Someone might be the greatest athlete in the world, but be conceited and mean. Then he or she is certainly not a success in the game of life.

Your crowning achievement will be shaping your character to resemble mine. This will be your masterpiece, and I will help you create it by guiding your hand and by interceding for you. As we work together on this venture, you will become more and more like Jesus.

Aim to be a person of integrity, someone who is honest, truthful, gentle, kind, and respectful of others. Love God and love all his people. If you achieve these things, then you will be a true champion. Your reward will not be in this world. However, in the next one you will shine like a star.

Entreat Mary to help you form virtues that make you more Christlike.

Good Thoughts

June 10

My child, your mind is a powerful gift that sets you apart from animals and governs the course of your life. All day long thoughts zip through your brain. Most likely, you seldom pay them much attention, much less study them. Outside influences infiltrate your mind with positive thoughts as well as negative ones. Other thoughts seem to arise out of nowhere.

Although some thoughts come to you unbidden, you can also control your mind. Focus on positive thoughts, what is good and beautiful. Uplifting thoughts improve your well-being and compel you to perform good actions. Be open to the inspirations that the Holy Spirit sends. As for the negative thoughts that depress you or that stimulate you to sin, drive them out as quickly as you shoo away mosquitoes.

Shield your mind from destructive thoughts by choosing your friends and your entertainment with care. Frequently direct your mind to dwell on your heavenly Father and me, your mother. When you do, you will be swathed in the peace I desire for you. Using your mind in the right way will also keep you close to me.

ભ *Reflect on the kind of thoughts that run through your mind. Ask Mary for the grace to control them.*

Mary's Presence

June 11

My child, you are never all alone. As you travel through life, I accompany you every step of the way. Together we skip or run through pleasant valleys and we trek over rough terrains and up steep mountains. I take my God-given role of being your mother very seriously, and I carry it out with all my heart. If only you were more aware of my loving presence!

When you meet a challenge and overcome it, I am relieved and happy for you. Your joy is echoed in me. When you suffer a tragedy, my heart aches for you. I want to clasp you close to me and comfort you. When you are confronted with a dilemma, I'm here to ask for the inspiration you need. When you are subjected to temptations, I'm with you to repel them.

I pray for you, dear one, and entreat God for the graces you need daily. I'm willing to do things for you that you might consider impossible. Realize how fond I am of you and talk to me often. I would like that very much.

ᥩ *Speak to Mary about your relationship with her and your desire to nurture it.*

Stay Focused

June 12

My child, your life is so full of activity that it makes me dizzy. You travel from one place to another. You keep appointments, and you visit friends and relatives. You carry out numerous projects for work or as hobbies. You clean your house and care for things. And on top of everything else, you plan meals every day.

Please take a breather from your hectic routine once in a while and recall the purpose of your life. You were made for the glory of God, and what you do on earth has bearing on your eternal life. So God firmly orders in Scripture, "Be still, and know that I am God!"[34] Leave behind the myriad distractions of your life and shift your attention to its underlying meaning. Be conscious of your preeminent goal, and then let it determine all of your decisions and actions.

I'm always concerned about your physical health, dear, but even more, your spiritual health. So periodically come apart from life's demands and responsibilities and rest. Reset your sights on God and what matters. Rely on me, darling, to help you see things as they really are.

CR *Talk to Mary about how you will take her advice.*

---

[34] Psalm 46:10

176

Mary's Love
Immaculate Heart of Mary

June 13
Saturday after the Solemnity of the Sacred Heart

My child, my heart beats with love for you, and so naturally I want what is best for you. For this reason I invite you to imitate me, your mother. You see, my heart is full of love for God and Jesus. It is pure, free from sin. When you love God very much, you will do anything for him, even hand over your life to him as I did. The more you love God, the more likely you will avoid sin that strains your relationship with him.

Loving God is automatic when you reflect on how greatly God loves you. He loved you first—before you even knew him. God says, "See, I have inscribed you on the palms of my hands."[35] You enjoy countless gifts that are signs of God's love. The most striking demonstration of God's love was the Incarnation. How could people ever dream of offending such a wonderful God?

I found out that loving God leads to intense joys as well as sometimes incredible sorrows. The joys, however, far outweigh the sorrows. And loving God culminates in joy that never ends.

CR *Talk over with Mary reasons you have for loving God.*

---

[35] Isaiah 49:16

Moral Discernment

June 14

My child, Christians who are discerning a choice and wish to keep in tune with God's great design are encouraged to ask themselves, "What would Jesus do?" I propose that you also ask, "What would Mary do?" After all, I was Jesus' first teacher!

When you are trying to decide what to do, you consult others. Why not come to me for advice, too? I know you very well, and I will point you in the right direction. Your decision will then be in keeping with Scripture and Church teaching. When you take me as a faithful guide for your life, you will be safe. I always chose to do the wise, right, and loving thing, even if it were challenging and seemingly impossible—like becoming an unwed mother when God asked this of me.

You can be sure that if you follow me, you also follow Jesus. And never fear. As you live out your choice, I will be your secure support every step of the way. Even if you choose wrongly, I won't desert you. Just hold fast to my hand and things will work out right.

ᙍ *Ask Mary to guide you in making the right decisions.*

Present Gifts

June 15

My child, stop right now and with me think of the treasures you possess. Is the sun shining? If it is, praise God. Do you have a roof over your head? Did you eat a delicious meal today, or will you? Is there a friend you can depend on for help? Are you in relatively good health? What other precious gems like these do you enjoy? All of them are gifts from your loving Father.

Now if the good God has taken care of you to this extent so far, be confident that God will do so in the future. Turn all your futile worries over to my hands, and I will dispose of them. Your fantasies of unfortunate events are often proved wrong anyway. From all eternity God meticulously and with love has laid marvelous plans for you. Relax and look forward with hope to the next gift that has your name on it.

Oh, and be sure to thank God for giving his mother to you to be your heavenly mother. I am one of his finest gifts, for my love for you is not only precious but permanent.

ॐ *Talk over with Mary some gifts you enjoy today.*

Weakness

June 16

My child, accept the fact that you are weak. You most likely have at least one physical disability like poor eyesight, poor hearing, or a bad heart that prevents you from living to the full. You also have moral disabilities like a hot temper or a bloated ego. Your limitations do not bar me or God from cherishing you. Actually, a mother often has a special place in her heart for her weakest child.

Don't fret about your lack of knowledge or skills, your inability to do great things, your laziness, or your tendency to sin. In a way, your weakness is an asset because it makes you depend more on Jesus. He said, "My grace is sufficient for you, for power is made perfect in weakness."[36] That should be reassuring. When you hand yourself over to Jesus through my hands, he will work through you to affect people in ways that may astound you. Even if you are bedridden and can only smile at people, don't fight your fate. That is enough.

Believe in Jesus and love others to the best of your ability. My son doesn't ask any more of you.

ᴄ℞ *Ask Mary to help you see what good you can do despite your limitations.*

---

[36] 2 Corinthians 12:9

A Safety Net

June 17

My child, sometimes you feel like Job. Misfortunes pile up until you can't bear it. You are depressed and petrified. You feel as though you have been shoved off a cliff and are falling down, down, down into darkness. Take heart, dearest, you will never hit bottom, for I am never far from you. I will rush in and catch you. I will hold you in my loving arms until the storms blow over. If you ask me, I will pray that your peace will be restored. I will tell you not to despair and give you reasons to go on living with hope in your heart. Changes occur unexpectedly, and when things are as bad as they can be, they can only improve.

Stay steadfast and unperturbed because the greatest change awaits you at the end of your life. If you have remained faithful to God, I will escort you into his glorious kingdom. There nothing will ever alarm you again, and you will have no cause to cry, except for tears of joy.

ᚷ *Has a calamity recently turned your life upside-down? Or do you fear an approaching one? If so, talk to Mary about your distress.*

Powerful Mother

June 18

My child, I like you to think of me as your sweet and gentle mother, for that is what I am. But remember, too, that I am powerful and known as Queen of Heaven and Earth. As the Mother of God, I have his ear and can bring about wonders on earth and for you. Trust me to always have your welfare at heart. Turn to me for help over and over until it becomes a habit. I will not disappoint you. I will never fail to plead to God for you.

Whenever you or your loved ones or friends are in trouble or bombarded by problems, call upon me. I will ask my son to deliver you from any trial and allay your concern. In the meantime, here is the best advice I can give you: Stay mindful of Jesus' presence deep in the cave of your heart. Visit him often and be refreshed by his love and energized by his power. When you do this, problems shrink and become more manageable. Then when God sees fit to answer my prayer for you, they will disappear.

No other person, neither man nor woman, has as much sway with God as I do, my darling.

℘ *Tell Mary about any situation that you would like her to pray for.*

Self-Pity

June 19

My child, you might have a dozen reasons to feel sorry for yourself, but don't! Drowning in self-pity is no way to live. It destroys the happiness I would like to have mark your days on earth. When I had to pack up and flee to Egypt with my baby, I could have felt sorry for myself. When I saw women in Nazareth walking with their brood of children and I had only one boy, I could have indulged in self-pity. But I resisted because self-pity is a danger that sours your life, does no good, and repels other people.

If someone expresses sympathy to you, instead of sighing and agreeing, "Woe is me," respond, "It could be worse" and change the subject. When you realize you are on the verge of self-pity, shift your focus away from your problems to your privileges. You have a heavenly mother who cares for you with all her heart. The almighty God dwells and acts within you. A glorious future of everlasting happiness has been prepared for you. Mentally reviewing the countless good things you have been blessed with and thanking God for them leaves no room for self-pity.

ⳍ *Ask Mary to obtain for you the grace to fend off self-pity despite your hardships.*

God's Steadfast Love

June 20

My child, you have no idea how much God loves you. When you consider your flaws and sins, you might surmise that his love comes and goes. But you would be absolutely wrong. His love is unswerving. On earth you can never fully comprehend how broad and deep God's love for you is. Now that I live in the celestial realm, I guarantee that God's love is infinite and beyond your wildest imagination. Not only does God love you unconditionally, but he loves you just as much today as he will in eternity.

I hope you will rest in the joy of this knowledge, dear. I assure you that my love for you is also strong and everlasting. I'm devoted to helping you love God now so that someday you will pass through heaven's gates, see him face-to-face, and know unequivocally how he feels about you.

ରଷ *What signs of God's love do you read in your life? Talk to Mary about them and your desire to grow in love for God.*

Hurdles

June 21

My child, when you peer into the coming week, you might see nothing but one hurdle after another. You might face difficult tasks, unpleasant meetings, and encounters with disagreeable people. Don't be daunted by these hurdles. You can be confident that one by one I will help you clear them safely and with ease.

When you are tied up in knots thinking about the problems you must surmount, you miss the beauty that those same days also hold for you. In fact, each hardship has a positive side. Open your eyes to the good outcome that God has thoughtfully attached to it. Maybe as you deal with the challenge, you become a stronger or a holier person. Perhaps you receive a new insight about yourself or others. You might meet a special person who will become a friend, an unexpected blessing for you.

Recall the times in the past that I boosted you successfully over a hurdle. Hold tight to my hand and you will run into this new week with a spring in your step and a smile on your face.

℞ *Tell Mary what difficulties you foresee in the next few days and ask her to stay by your side.*

Self-Discipline

June 22

My child, doing what God expects of you—and most likely what you expect of yourself—requires discipline. But it is more enticing to coast along an easy road than hiking up mountains. You can surrender to the lure of pleasures like sweets and long naps or deny yourself. When you don't feel like going to Mass, you can skip it or master yourself. You can do a slipshod job or put your best into it. You can stubbornly hold a grudge or grit your teeth and extend forgiveness. For these and similar matters, the choice is yours.

Ask me and I will obtain the grace for you to take yourself in hand and overcome a natural tendency to take the easy way. If you practice self-control often enough, it will become second nature to you. Then when you face a situation that calls for prodigious effort, you will have the spiritual muscle to rise to the occasion. Imagine the self-discipline I needed to follow Jesus to Calvary when my whole being rebelled against it. Let me help you strengthen your backbone so you can be proud of yourself.

cs *Talk to Mary about an area in which you need more self-discipline.*

The Holy Spirit

June 23

My child, pray to the Holy Spirit. This Third Person of the Trinity is often neglected, which is a shame. At the Last Supper, my son said he would ask the Father to send the Holy Spirit to be your Advocate or helper and dwell in you forever.[37] Take advantage of this marvelous gift. The all-powerful and all-wise Spirit of Jesus is right within you. Ask this Person to teach you more about God, to guide you when you are in a quandary, and to send the gentle breeze of divine inspiration when you need an idea. You can't have a stronger, more reliable life companion than God residing in your heart. Not even I can compare, for I'm not a goddess, but a human being like you.

Through the Holy Spirit, I brought the Son of God into the world. Through the grace of the Holy Spirit, you can be another Christ in your world. As you go through this day's ups and downs, think about the Holy Spirit living in you. Call upon this constant Friend to come to your aid and then watch the results. I have a hunch that you may be pleasantly surprised.

CR *Tell Mary about your relationship with the Holy Spirit. Ask her to help you deepen it.*

---

[37] John 14:16–17

Contemplation

June 24

My child, contemplation is the highest form of prayer, and so you might assume that it is difficult and reserved for the very holy. No, you do not have to be a great saint to enjoy contemplation. You don't achieve it, for it is purely a gift from God. This prayer is as simple as gazing into the face of a loved one, and it brings about the same deep joy. When Jesus and I lived under the same roof, at times we wouldn't speak. I just looked at him and delighted in being with him.

When you behold a breathtaking scene in nature, you stand quietly in awe. The prayer of contemplation is similar. You become still and quiet and then rest in the knowledge that you are in the presence of God, who is looking at you with tremendous love. You might feel as though nothing is happening, but God's grace is at work in you. Any minute he might grant you the grace of contemplation.

I will pray that you engage in quiet prayer often. When you do contemplate God, I will be next to you, also contemplating God. The difference will be that I actually behold God face-to-face, a destiny I wish for you with all my heart, dearest.

℘ *Talk to Mary about how to improve your prayer life.*

Self-Worth

June 25

My child, things occur that make you doubt your self-worth. You don't fit in with a certain group. When people recount an event, they remark, "Oh, were you there, too?" You propose an idea, which is ignored until someone else repeats it and is given the credit for it. You're overlooked for a promotion. Or someone makes a scathing remark either about you or something you've done. Experiences like these sting and make you wonder if something is wrong with you.

Never fear. You have inestimable value, although sometimes people don't recognize it. To me you are a unique and therefore special child of God. You are beautiful in my eyes, and I treasure my relationship with you as your heavenly mother. Please don't ever let other people thoughtlessly or maliciously whittle away your self-confidence. Focus on the many talents and blessings you enjoy and others do not, and thank God for them. When people wound your self-esteem, come immediately to me. I will tell you to stand tall and remind you with a hug that I love you for who you are.

ᘓ *Ask Mary for the grace to see yourself as God and she both see you.*

A Merciful Heart

June 26

My child, extending mercy to others is the key to the kingdom of God. My son told a parable about two kinds of people. One group shows love by feeding the hungry, giving drink to the thirsty, welcoming the stranger, clothing the naked, caring for the sick, and visiting prisoners. On judgment day Jesus will welcome these people into his Father's kingdom. The other group who failed to perform those acts of mercy will be doomed to eternal punishment.

You carry out these works of mercy for your family members just as I did. Sometimes you extend your love for the needy outside your home. That is good. I urge you to do more if you can. Your days may be crammed with numerous tasks. You may feel irritated when you are bombarded by pleas for help from different organizations. Nevertheless, I ask you to expand your heart and show even more love.

It won't be easy to balance your obligations and additional acts of mercy. Ask me to help you do this in a way that doesn't make your life more stressful. I long for the day when you will join me in our Father's kingdom.

ᦤ *Talk with Mary about acts of mercy you could take on.*

When You Need Assistance
Our Lady of Perpetual Help

June 27

My child, I want to help you face each day's challenges. One of my favorite titles is Our Lady of Perpetual Help. In the icon by that name, I hold the child Jesus. He is looking up at an angel carrying a cross and nails. This vision terrifies Jesus. He grasps my thumb with both hands and has run to me so fast that one sandal fell off and dangles from his foot. But I am gazing not at my son, but at you.

Not only in the icon but in real life, too, I am fondly gazing at you, and I read your heart. Just as Jesus found a safe haven in me whenever he was frightened as a child in Nazareth, you will too.

I urge you to come to me for shelter in my arms when you need aid, comfort, and encouragement. At times you are overcome with fear or dread. Maybe you await test results, your loved one is missing, or you suffer from insomnia. Run to me for help. I'm available for you and eager to calm your fears and bring you peace. Always. You too are my precious child.

ଓ *Share your fears with Mary and let her quell them.*

Strength

June 28

My child, when life seems unbearable, when you suffer a tragedy that shakes your whole being, when you are sick and tired of your grueling job, or when you are tortured by temptations, have faith. God promised that you will not be tested beyond your strength. That is because you have supernatural power to draw on.

Besides the graces of your baptism and the help of the Holy Spirit dwelling in you, I am here with you. With tender care I coax you to endure any trial with stamina and resilience. Do you remember how God saw the Israelites through their many trials in the desert? Do you recall how God upheld me during my sufferings? Lean on me. I can obtain the same grace of strength from God for you. Just ask.

With my assistance, you can face the future with hope. Know that no mountain is too high and no river is too deep to impede or halt your progress to eternal life when I accompany you. If you are overwhelmed by sorrow, grab my hand and hold on tight.

ᴄᴈ *Entreat Mary to be your companion and to pray for you during any hardship you face now or in the future.*

Love Bursts

June 29

My child, God delights in sprinkling your days with little favors. I recognized his hand in my life often. Once when I was mending a hole in Joseph's tunic, I had just enough thread to finish. Another time at the market I got a great bargain on olives right before they ran out. Then there was the day my morning began with a double rainbow arched over our village. You too have had such fortunate experiences, but maybe you didn't give God the credit for them.

As you go through your day, watch for God's courtesies. Maybe you are in the right place at the right time for something wonderful. Maybe you meet a friend from the past or you miraculously avoid a serious accident. Such happenings are not mere coincidences.

I will help keep you alert for God's special blessings. When one of God's love bursts comes along, I will nudge you to open your eyes to it. Our good God is not too big to show love in tiny details. You will make me happy by showing him love in return by little deeds. Surprise him.

ന *Review the past day with Mary and detect evidences of God's love for you.*

Dealing with Opponents

June 30

My child, you may have experienced striving for a goal that you deemed good, but then a person gets in your way and jeopardizes your efforts. This happens to the best of people. I recall how religious leaders tried to thwart Jesus' ministry. When this happens to you, try calmly reasoning with your opponent. If this fails to move him or her, entreat me to help you by asking God to change the person's mind. If your opponent still stands steadfastly against what you propose, I can ask the Holy Spirit to inspire you with a way to bypass that obstacle and achieve your goal.

It could be that nothing works and you are stymied. Be ready to gracefully accede to God's superior plan, trusting that in some mysterious way, your failure will all be for the best. Guard your heart from any bitter feelings toward the person who opposed you. Look to me for help in treating him or her like a friend. Keep in mind that although my son's opponents appeared to win, a great number of people are following him today.

ℚ *Is someone blocking your way as you reach for a worthy goal? Ask Mary for assistance in overcoming your problem.*

July

Precious Blood

July 1

My child, I was with Jesus at his circumcision when his blood was first shed. Even then I cringed to know the pain he felt. It was hard to believe that God would undergo that. A million times worse, was the shedding of Jesus' blood at the end of his life on earth. What a shock on the way to Calvary to see my son's face caked with blood and his clothes soaked with it! Then looking up at him on the cross, in anguish I watched drops of his blood fall to the ground. Finally, it was over when with a thrust of a lance, blood and water streamed from his side. My son's blood was the price paid for your eternal life.

At Mass you become one with Jesus when you consume the sacred bread, his body, and sip the sacred wine, his blood. Don't try to understand this mystery. Accept it on faith, just as I accepted the mystery of my son's suffering and death. Jesus and I both surrendered our lives to God for your sake, my dear child. Do you need any more proof of the tremendous love we have for you?

ଔ *Talk to Mary about your love for her son.*

God's Marvelous Deeds

July 2

My child, every breath you take and every heartbeat is sustained by God. Likewise, whatever good you do is the result of God's action in you. On the day my cousin Elizabeth called me blessed among women, I praised God, saying, "the Mighty One has done great things for me."[38] God is the source of my holiness and any good that I accomplish. I am not a goddess, but a created human being like you. Both of us have been showered with gifts by our magnanimous Father.

Think of the innumerable wonderful things God has done for you. You might start with the fact that God called you out of nothingness into being! The good people who enrich your life, the awesome wonders of the natural world, your talents, and successes — all are orchestrated by your heavenly Father, who loves you deeply. Remember to share the credit for your gifts and triumphs with him. Join me in praising God now on earth and look forward to praising God with me forever in heaven, praying, "the Mighty One has done great things for me."

Talk to Mary about some great things God has done for you.

---

[38] Luke 1:46

A Mother's Understanding

July 3

My child, don't be surprised if people misjudge you, give the impression that they think you are strange, or criticize you. Some days you feel as though no one understands you. This frustrates and depresses you. It makes you think that you are all alone in the world. You long for a friend who knows you as you really are and accepts you.

Do not lose sight of me. I, your heavenly mother, completely understand you. I know your intentions, your motivations, your good qualities, and your potential. I also know your weaknesses, but like any mother, I can make excuses for you!

You are never completely alone because I am near you day in and day out. What's more, no matter what you do, I will never abandon you, and you can never run away from me, dearest. Breathe deeply and surrender to me. Let my love flow over you and wipe out the sense of not being understood. As I enfold you in my warm embrace, that uncomfortable feeling will be replaced by joy.

ভ *Do you need a friend other than Mary? Implore her to pray God to send you a good companion.*

Singing as Prayer

July 4

My child, I love to sing. When Jesus was an infant, I sang him to sleep with lullabies. Later I taught him the childhood songs Jewish boys and girls sang and the traditional songs we sang on Jewish feasts. On the way to the Temple and during the services, we sang psalms. There is something I find so satisfying in lifting my voice in song to praise God.

You might not have the greatest voice in the world, but God is pleased when you join in the singing in church. A sung prayer takes more effort that a recited one. I like to hear you sing to me not only in church but when we are alone. Don't be shy. Some people in love sing to their loved ones. Singing Marian hymns shows your love for me. I especially like to hear the Magnificat sung, for I prayed it to acknowledge all that God had done for me and my people.

I hope that someday you and I will join with the choirs of angels in singing praise endlessly to our heavenly Father.

ೞ *Talk to Mary about your attitude toward singing and how you might use your voice to praise God.*

Trust in the Face of Enormous Tasks
July 5

My child, you may be challenged by an endeavor that seems beyond your capabilities. You doubt that you possess the knowledge, skills, strength, or patience to carry it out. Your intimidating task might be having your first child, being appointed to a high position, or going through weeks of rehabilitation. Although you may lack certain qualifications, you have one strong asset to offset any deficits, and that is my unfailing assistance.

Trust me to see you successfully fulfill any responsibility that looms before you like a gigantic mountain. I'll be holding your arm securely, as securely as I held Jesus when he was beginning to walk. We'll go one step at a time. During your venture, you might take a few tumbles, but in the end you will be all right.

Whenever you feel as though it is impossible to go on and you want to quit, turn to me and ask my help. You can be confident that I, your ever-loving, full-time mother, will manage to obtain the graces you need to conquer your fears and complete your task. Count on celebrating your ultimate victory with me.

ᖴ *Are you apprehensive about an upcoming task? Tell Mary about it and ask her help.*

Mistakes

July 6

My child, you often make embarrassing mistakes that you regret. That is a normal part of the human condition. Perhaps you unintentionally make a remark that hurts someone's feelings. Maybe you forget to attend an important meeting or you omit a necessary ingredient in a recipe. Whatever your error, large or small, don't obsess about it. Rather, pick yourself up, dust yourself off, and walk on. I watch you closely and can assure you that you do a great many more things right than you do wrong. So refuse to allow mistakes to chip away at your self-respect.

I suggest, though, that you spend a little more time thinking before you speak or act. Don't do things impulsively. Haste sometimes leads to bad decisions that harm you or others. I'm remembering King Herod's rash promise to give the dancing girl anything she wished, an act that resulted in the martyrdom of John, my cousin Elizabeth's son. I don't think any less of you, dear, after you make a foolish mistake. My compassionate love encircles you like a cloak that you cannot remove.

ᚲᚱ *Talk to Mary about your intention to avoid mistakes. Ask her help in slowing down.*

A Thankful Heart

July 7

My child, cultivate a thankful heart and you will smile more often than you frown. When you are swept up in the whirlwind of activities each day, you might be oblivious to the many blessings God generously bestows on you. Make a point of noticing them and saying thank you. Each time you do makes you more aware of God and draws you nearer to him. Besides, saying thank you to God is a prayer that glorifies him.

If your heart is full of gratitude, the difficulties you encounter will be like little pinpricks. As you become more sensitive to our heavenly Father's love for you, your trust in him will expand. You will realize that God will not let you down but supply the rush of graces you need to meet any challenge. This conviction leads to great peace and joy.

In particular, when you implore me to pray for an intention and you receive it, you naturally thank me. Remember, dear, to also thank God, for he is the one who responds to your request through me. I thank him too!

ᑲ *Ask Mary to help you to be more conscious of God's blessings during the day.*

Patience

July 8

My child, your heavenly Father is eager to answer your prayers if in the big picture they are for the benefit of all. At times, however, God appears to turn a deaf ear to you, and you wonder if something is wrong. Realize that God lives in eternity, which is quite different from time. Scripture says, "With the Lord one day is like a thousand years, and a thousand years are like one day."[39] Look how long my people waited before the Messiah arrived. Centuries rolled by. And my son said he would return to earth, but again centuries have passed. Trust me, God is faithful and eventually keeps his promise.

The psalmist urged, "Wait for the LORD; be strong, and let your heart take courage!"[40] I say the same thing to you, dearest. When God doesn't answer your prayers right away, don't give up hope. And don't quit praying. Just wait patiently. You might occasionally tug on my mantle and ask me to remind God of your request. I'm always happy to intercede for you.

✎ *Share with Mary intentions for which you have been praying for a long time.*

---

[39] 2 Peter 3:8

[40] Psalm 27:1

Longing for Peace
Our Lady, Queen of Peace

July 9

My child, the world is wracked with wars, political parties within countries are at odds, families are torn apart by disagreements, and sometimes your own heart is in turmoil. This turbulence is not how our loving God created the human race to be. It's the result of sin.

When Jesus was born, angels declared, "Peace, among those whom he favors!."[41] The sacrifice of Jesus healed the rupture between God and the human race. My son brought about peace. He is the Prince of Peace. I, his mother, can be a vessel of peace wherever there is conflict. Ask me to entreat God to put out the fires that rage. Let the healing balm of peace flow over the world, dousing the flames of anger and hatred.

When you are upset, dear, come to me and let me soothe your troubled heart. If you are anxious about the future, I will assure you that it is in God's loving hands. If guilt weighs you down, find relief in the sacrament of peace. As your mother, I am concerned about you. I want you to sleep well and have a healthy appetite. I want you to be at peace here and hereafter.

ℭℛ *Talk to Mary about anything disturbing your peace.*

---

[41] Luke 2:14

Anticipating God's Action

July 10

My child, you can wake up expecting to have a good day. For one thing, I will be tenderly watching over you, ready to spring into action whenever you need me. Moreover, your heavenly Father painstakingly plans every detail of your life. You can count on him to have special treasures buried in each day for you. Some of these you will immediately recognize as gems. Others will appear covered in dirt at first but will turn out to be gems as well. Be on the lookout to discover these treasures.

Knowing that one or more blessings await you puts you in a good mood. You start the day off right instead of grumpily. Then during the day, you are less susceptible to temptations and better equipped to deal with problems. Best of all, when you are in a good frame of mind, you are more apt to be a blessing for others by treating them with love and respect.

And so, dearest, each morning, hold onto my hand and let's go forward as though embarking on an exciting adventure.

Talk to Mary about your desire to have a positive attitude each new day.

Glory on Earth

July 11

My child, earth abounds with hints of heaven. You look out your window and see sunlight bathing the top of the tree across the street, and you are swept away by the sight. That is a glimpse of glory. You behold a dazzling rainbow stretched across a dark grey sky, and a burst of joy overcomes you. That is a taste of glory. You catch sight of a loved one gazing at you with a special tenderness, and you are moved to tears. That is a little of what heaven is like.

For me, heaven on earth was living with Jesus for most of my life. He is with you too every day and all day long, although not in the flesh. Be aware of the flashes of heaven you are privy to now, and savor the abiding presence of Jesus with you. It won't be long before you stand at the gates of the actual heaven. With every fiber of my being I hope that you will be admitted quickly to live with Jesus and me for years without end. Then your joy will be complete, and so will mine, dearest.

ℭ *Speak to Mary about your longing for heaven.*

Shortcomings

July 12

My dear, even saints have their flaws, so don't be surprised that you do. Some shortcomings you can do nothing about, for example, being small in stature or not being able to carry a tune. You just have to accept them as your lot in life. Other flaws, however, you can control and even eliminate, such as a quick temper or being self-centered. When you realize—or someone points out—that you possess a manageable flaw, no doubt you wish to fix it. Enlist my help. As your mother, I desire your happiness and being the best person you can be increases that.

None of your shortcomings are a barrier to my love for you. In fact, they may make you more endearing to me. My favorite pot at home had a little crack in it, but I used it all of the time. Be content to be who you are. You do not have to be jealous of others, not even if they are holier than you. Look into my face and read there that I treasure you. I assure you that God can work wonders through you despite your shortcomings.

‽ *Talk to Mary about any shortcomings you would like to deal with and ask her help.*

A Saving Beauty
Mary, Mystical Rose

July 13

My child, if you love roses, you are not alone. I do too. Their beauty and lovely fragrance make them the most popular flower all over the world. People present them to loved ones, the sick, and people who achieved success. I'm touched when you offer me roses, placing them by my image. I know that is a sign of your love for me. I would like to shower you with dozens of red roses!

My title mystical rose is fitting. Because my body and soul are in heaven, I am now mystical, which is why I'm invisible to you. I truly am real though, and I can see you. You might wonder how a flower with thorns can represent me. Those thorns are beautiful to me because they stand for my sacrifice that enabled you to enjoy everlasting life.

Roses are called the queen of flowers, and I too am a queen. Not only am I blessed among women, I am the queen of heaven and earth. What matters most to me, my dear, is that you regard me not so much as queen, but as your devoted mother.

☙ *Speak with Mary about why the rose symbolizes her. Place a rose before her image.*

A Calloused Heart?

July 14

My child, I hope you never have a calloused heart. The Israelites were accused of being hardhearted, and rightly so. They did not listen to God. Don't be stubborn like them. Imitate me, your loving mother, who surrendered completely to God's will. Be open to God's words and live by them. They are intended to bring you joy. Both God and I want only your happiness.

Perhaps you do everything God says with one exception. It could be you refuse to love a certain person, or maybe you succumb to a bad habit. That means one area of your heart is calloused, and a word of God ricochets off of it. Even only one calloused part is not good enough, dear. I wish you to have a heart that is totally soft and tender, beating with love for God, for others, and for yourself.

One remedy for a calloused heart is to develop callouses on your knees. I urge you to pray to me often. I will be happy to ask my son, the divine physician, for the graces that will cure you and give you a heart like mine.

଼ *Talk to Mary about any of God's words that are not penetrating your heart.*

Petitions and Presence

July 15

My child, every day various concerns weigh on your heart. A friend is ill, a family member is deployed to a dangerous land, or you face a job interview. You hope that situations like these turn out for the good. You can do more than hope. I invite you to ask my help in any trying situation. I am always more than willing to place your request before your heavenly Father and plead for you.

Realize, though, I desire your time with me to be spent not only praying for help, but in nurturing our relationship. I wish you to come to know me the way I know you, dear one. Sit quietly and be present to me. Visualize me sitting with you. Enjoy my constant company and speak to me. Pray prayers that others composed, or tell me whatever you wish in your own words. Mull over Gospel passages about incidents in my life in order to learn more about me. Talk to me about them. Reflectively read books and articles about me. By doing these things, you will grow closer to me because your eyes will be opened to the immense love I have for you.

❧ *Share with Mary what is going on in your life right now.*

The Interior Life
Our Lady of Mount Carmel

July 16

My child, you care for your physical life by eating, exercising, playing, visiting doctors, and resting. Much of your time is spent engaged in the material world. A vital part of you, however, is spiritual, and you must see that your interior life thrives too. Allow me, your heavenly mother, to show you how.

My whole life on earth centered around God. My thoughts frequently flew to him, and I spoke with him, who lived in me by faith. In my heart I pondered his wonderful, mysterious deeds. Most likely you are not called to be a contemplative monk or nun. Still, in the midst of your busy days, either mentally or physically draw apart from the world. Sink down into the abyss of your being and there encounter the living God. Reflect on the blessings he has shown you. Nurture his divine life in you through the sacraments. Aim to be as one with God as I was. That is the ultimate goal I wish for you, for I desire your total happiness, my dear.

ᘒ *Wearing the scapular of Our Lady of Mount Carmel is a sign of an intention to live an interior life. Talk to Mary about wearing a cloth one or a medal yourself.*

A Humble Soul
Humility of the Blessed Virgin Mary

July 17

My child, God loves humble souls who are not self-centered and puffed up with pride. They see themselves honestly as weak human beings dependent on God. Jesus, whose humility was outstanding, said, "Learn from me; for I am gentle and humble in heart."[42] My humility attracted God. In my Magnificat prayer I said, "He has looked with favor on the lowliness of his servant." I knew that I was an ordinary girl of no account in the world. God knew my heart and was confident that I would agree to his will. He was right. I didn't stubbornly argue against his plan for me, but submitted to it.

When you are humble, you are willing to be God's servant as I was. What is God asking you to do? If it is something intimidating, ask me to help you. When you are humble, you graciously serve others. After I knew I was to be the Mother of God, I could have expected people to wait on me. Instead I spent months caring for my pregnant cousin Elizabeth. When you know someone needs help, ask yourself what I would do.

ଔ *Talk to Mary about signs that you are becoming humble.*

---

[42] Matthew 11:29

Simplicity

July 18

My child, your life is quite complicated and sometimes chaotic. You are surrounded by gadgets, possessions, and noise. You are pulled in many directions by appointments, meetings, and responsibilities. My heart goes out to you when I see you stressed and frantic. That is not the kind of abundant life my son came to give.

Can you streamline your life so that you can focus on what really matters? You will live for an eternity, but you have only a limited number of years to serve God and love others on earth. With my assistance you can make the most of them.

Break the hold that things have on you. Wean yourself away from what is not necessary. Go through your closets and storage rooms, and I will help you decide what to keep, dispose of, or give away. Listen to me prompting you to say no to taking on extra projects or work. Once you free yourself from many of the trappings that clog your day, you will be able to breathe. And what I especially look forward to: you will have more time to spend with me and my son.

ଓ *Review with Mary what possessions and commitments you can do away with in order to live a simpler, happier life.*

Stillness

July 19

My child, often you are on the go running errands and engaged in a flurry of activities. Your mind races with thoughts of what you must do yet. To stay healthy and sane, dear, every once in a while you need to stop everything and be still. That is when you come into contact with the very source of your life. Jesus was born in the course of the night when the world was quietly at rest. Likewise he will make himself known to you when you drop everything and sit still.

Jesus speaks softly. He doesn't pound on the door of your heart. The prophet Elijah heard God's voice not in wind or earthquake or roaring fire, but when there was sheer silence.[43] By sitting still, you will be able to hear God and me whispering to you. As you spend time in peaceful stillness communing with us, don't fret about other things on your agenda. They will all be completed in God's good time if it is his will. I will see to it. The graces you gain will more than make up for your "lost" time.

ᘏ *Talk to Mary about a plan for scheduling time for prayerful relaxation. Ask her help in sticking to it.*

---

[43] 1 Kings 19:11–12

The Divine Potter

July 20

My child, God sent the prophet Jeremiah to the potter's house and told him that Israel was like clay in his hands. Isn't that a beautiful figure of speech? You are like clay in God's hands. He originally fashioned you into a unique person and is still working on you, shaping you tenderly and expertly with his gentle hands. Be supple clay, dearest, and cooperate with him. You do not always understand God's intentions, but trust this divine artist as I did.

In Nazareth I had a number of pots that held water carried from the well and stored grain and other foods. None of these pots, not even the prettiest, was solely for decoration. They were all useful. Offer yourself to God to be used as he wishes. I will help you not to fear his plans nor to be skeptical of them.

Let yourself be filled to the brim with God's life, grace, and then take it to others in the forms of light, hope, and love. If you do this, you will be like one of my favorite clay pots!

ৎ *Talk over with Mary ways that God may be calling you to be useful.*

A Constant Companion

July 21

My child, I am with you day and night, even when you are not thinking of me or speaking to me. I watch over you, help you as you grow, and wish the best for you as much as I did for my son. I am glad when you are happy, and when you are upset, I am concerned. It saddens me when you don't keep in touch with me for a long stretch of time. But when you reconnect with me, my heart rejoices.

Each day holds its share of tasks, challenges, and temptations for you. Some of these are annoying stumbling stones; others are heavy boulders. They are all part of your trial on earth. By successfully managing them, you will reach your desired destination, heaven.

Through every difficulty you encounter, I'm at your side, ready to clear the way for you to peace and joy. Reach out to me and take hold of my strong hand. With me you will walk safely and boldly along the way.

❧ *Thank Mary for the tender care she gives you.*

Discipleship

July 22

My child, a zealous Christian steadfastly stays close to Jesus like Mary of Magdala did. After Jesus healed Mary, she joined his disciples, supporting the group financially and preparing meals. I admired Mary for that and was grateful to her. She followed my son to the cross. I appreciated her support there and drew strength from her presence. Because Mary was at the tomb on Easter morning, she saw the risen Jesus and was sent to deliver the good news to the apostles.

I urge you to imitate Mary's ardent love for Jesus. He healed you of sin and can heal you in other ways too. If you stay close to him day after day, you will be greatly rewarded. Be aware of Jesus around you and within you. Speak to him. When hardships come your way, unite them to his sufferings for the world's redemption. Receive Jesus in the Eucharist often. Imagine my joy at receiving him for the first time through Peter. That same privilege is yours.

I can't even describe how much I love you. My constant prayer is that you draw nearer to Jesus. That is the greatest thing I can do for you, dearest.

ભ *Speak to Mary about your desire to deepen your friendship with Jesus.*

Grace for the Asking
Mother of Divine Grace

July 23

My child, Jesus is the fountain of all graces, but he has chosen to have them flow through my hands. I am like a treasurer, and I wish to dispense plentiful graces to you, my beloved. Ask me to intercede for you. Are you fighting temptation? Ask me for the grace to stand firm. Are you struggling in prayer? Ask me for the grace to be fervent and persistent. Are you snared by a problem? Ask me for the grace to free yourself. Are you facing a dilemma? Ask me for the grace to make the right decision. Are you in turmoil because of a certain situation? Ask me for the grace of peace.

A thousand graces are yours for the asking. It would give me great pleasure to persuade my son to let me impart to you the ones you need or desire. Whenever you realize that your prayer has been answered, you might see me wink at you! Making you happy is one of my favorite occupations in heaven. Take advantage of it. I'm privileged to be able to shower on you as many graces as you ask.

CB *What grace do you most desire today? Ask Mary to obtain it for you.*

Laughter

July 24

My child, when something strikes you as funny, you burst out laughing. God gave us humans a sense of humor that distinguishes us from animals and makes life more enjoyable. We Jews have a proverb: "What soap is to the body, laughter is to the soul." I loved to hear Baby Jesus laughing when I tickled him or when Joseph tossed him up into the air. Often our little house rang with laughter when Joseph came home from work and related a ridiculous thing that occurred.

I like to hear you laugh too because it means you are at peace. In the book of Proverbs, because a woman is strong and capable, "she laughs at the time to come."[44] Joy is also a sign of holiness. As this day wears on, look for the incongruous and humorous. Find the humor in trying circumstances. Laugh freely. Laugh at yourself—at your pretensions, peccadillos, and predicaments. Make others laugh, even at your own expense. Tell a joke or play a harmless prank on someone. Causing laughter is a form of charity.

As you laugh, dear, I will be laughing with you.

ଘ *Ask Mary to help you to see the funny side of frustrating situations.*

---

[44] Proverbs 31:25

Reputations

July 25

My child, most people desire a good reputation, to be highly thought of by others. Reputations are as fragile as glass. A few words can easily damage them. How hurt I was when word spread through our village that my Jesus was crazy or even possessed. That slander turned our neighbors' minds against him, even though they had long experienced his goodness and kindness.

My son is not happy when people ruin reputations by spreading allegations, either well founded or false. Their malicious words may be motivated by jealousy. Some slanderers put people down so that they themselves might rise in others' estimation. I hope you never feel that you have to malign another person. You are always precious in my eyes.

Have you ever been slandered or the victim of harmful gossip? If so, you are like Jesus. Take heart. God and I know the truth about you and your actions. We are the only ones you really have to please. Let me wrap you in my protective mantle so that slurs slide off you harmlessly and fall to the ground.

ଔ *Talk to Mary about any time your reputation has been attacked.*

Mothers and Fathers
Saints Joachim and Anne

July 26

My child, from all eternity your all-wise God chose your specific mother and father to be your earthly parents. My parents, Joachim and Anne, were a devout couple who provided for me from the day I was born until I left our family home. In their loving care, I learned about my heavenly Father and how to please him.

Your parents, too, not only brought you into the world but fed and clothed you and set you on the right path to the best of their ability. They might not be saints, but cherish them. Overlook their faults and make allowances for the mistakes they might have made in raising you. Express your gratitude by your words and actions, and also in creative ways.

Like other human beings, I experienced the death of my mother and father. Knowing that I'd never see them again on earth was painful. But because of their grandson, Jesus, I could look forward to being reunited with them in heaven. You can hope to be with your parents and other family members in the next world too. Know that I care for them with the same loving devotion I care for you.

ɔ *Talk to Mary about your mother and father.*

A Garden of Virtues

July 27

My child, virtues are good qualities that I hope flourish in the garden of your soul. Humility is the little violet. It appears when you are unassuming and honest about yourself. Obedience is the carnation that bows to the wind. Your salvation depends on moving with the inspirations of the Holy Spirit. Simplicity is the daisy. Its beauty lies in centering on God alone. Hope is the sunflower that always looks up to God even when skies are overcast. Love is the beautiful rose that uplifts everyone who beholds it. Faith is the sturdy oak in the middle of the garden.

Let me help you tend your garden. Graces I procure for you will rain down from heaven and strengthen your virtues. Together you and I will root out the weeds of vices or sins that choke the lovely flowers. Selfishness, greed, and unbridled ambition have no business growing in you. Producing a gorgeous garden is hard work I admit. You need determination and persistence. The more virtues blooming in your soul, the more you will resemble me, my dear, and the more pleasing you will be to our heavenly Father, who absolutely loves flowers.

ଔ *What virtue would you like to especially practice this month? Tell Mary and ask her assistance.*

Unwelcome Consequences

July 28

My child, sometimes you do a good deed with the best intentions, and it goes wrong. For example, you compliment someone, but your words are misinterpreted as an insult, or you give someone a helping hand and only make matters worse. Maybe you return a lost item and are accused of stealing it. When these kinds of things happen, you are deflated and wish you had never made the overture. Let me heal your wounded heart.

Have no regrets. I know what you had in mind, and I'm proud of you. I love you for your kind gestures to others. I can also assure you that God blesses you for your attempts to do good even if people don't understand or appreciate them. He can turn your acts into gold. Remember that God sent his Son out of love for us. My Jesus performed acts of love one after another, yet he was rejected and killed.

Don't be discouraged from performing good deeds in the future no matter how many times they turn out badly. Your reward is waiting for you in heaven, and so am I.

cઝ *Talk to Mary about a time your good deed backfired.*

When Life Is a Maze

July 29

My child, at times you feel as though you are walking through a maze full of twists and turns. You long to escape but search in vain for the exit. You make wrong turns and find yourself going around in circles. You become confused, frustrated, and perhaps on the verge of panicking.

There's no need to be afraid. I am so very fond of you, and I wish to relieve you from feeling lost and helpless. I have a bird's eye view of your situation and can free you from your predicament. Turn to me with confidence, darling, and ask me for enlightenment as to what decisions to make.

After you do so, the Holy Spirit will slip an inspiration into your mind, you will encounter a person who guides you to the right path, or you will read or hear something that provides the direction you need. In whatever form it comes, the assistance that leads you out of the maze is a grace that I, your mother, have obtained for you. Then you can breathe easily again and enjoy your freedom.

ᘏ *Is something causing you to feel trapped? Talk to Mary about it.*

Giving Compliments

July 30

My child, complimenting someone is a little act of love. It creates a warm, happy feeling in people when their achievement or personal quality is recognized and acknowledged. My son was lavish with compliments. He praised a Roman centurion for his faith and the woman who washed his feet with her tears for her great love.

Sometimes you mentally note a person's good point but neglect to communicate that you are aware of it. Today let me help you give compliments. Keep an eye out for someone who deserves one. Perhaps a store clerk responds calmly to an irate customer, or a coworker walks in with a new, flattering hairdo. Your compliment must be sincere. Then express it in such a way that the person is pleased.

Many prayers and hymns to me contain compliments. In them you address me as beautiful, pure and holy, good, and gracious. I take these compliments as tokens of your love for me. In return, I want you to know that I'm aware of your good qualities and achievements, even those you do not realize! A day will come when I will inform you of them and tell you how proud I am of you.

ભ *Talk to Mary about people you could compliment today. Put your compliments in writing to make them more impactful.*

Taking a Break

July 31

My child, whatever is going on in your life or whatever is going on in the world right now, step back and stay with me a while. Clear the past from your mind and cease imagining how the future will unfold. Just be quiet and for a few minutes enjoy the thought that I love you deeply and care for you. Imagine my maternal love washing over you like a warm shower. Feel my embrace and listen to my heart beating with love for you.

Realize that my love for you is only a faint reflection of the profound love your heavenly Father bears toward you. God loves you because God is love. He created you in his image, and you are his beloved child. You belong to him. With infinite care he has created a blueprint for your life.

God and I are always with you and are involved in your life, even though you don't perceive us with your eyes or ears. Never doubt our love for you and our strong desire to see you safely home with us someday.

␣ *Ask Mary to pray for the grace that you live worthy of the love she and God have for you.*

August

God's Kingdom

August 1

My child, I had a special role in God's kingdom, but so do you. God placed you in this time and country, with certain people, and in circumstances unlike anyone else. He depends on you to do your part in making his kingdom come on earth. If you don't, no one will substitute for you.

Like me, you are privileged to join in God's great enterprise. Through your baptism you were called to this task. It is not an easy one. You bring about the kingdom by the witness of your life. But you and I know that in some instances there is a gap between what you believe and how you live. You also promote the kingdom by working for peace and justice. You might possibly devote more time to that undertaking. When spreading the kingdom is risky, you may be reluctant to do it.

Let me be your partner. If you rely on me, you will have the courage and resourcefulness to carry out your God-given role successfully. Your efforts will not be sterile, and my son will be pleased with you.

ભ *Tell Mary ways that she can assist you in moving your corner of the world closer to the kingdom.*

Heavenly Visitors
Our Lady, Queen of Angels

August 2

My child, I hope you believe in angels as most people have through the centuries. I assure you that angels are as real as you. However, since they are pure spirits, you can't see them. It was the Angel Gabriel who visited me to deliver God's invitation to be his mother. Angels appeared in the sky the night Jesus was born.

Currently I live surrounded by hosts of majestic angels. With the choirs of angels, I glorify God, our creator. Even though they are vastly superior beings, I'm their queen in virtue of being God's Mother. Together with your Guardian Angel, I watch over you day and night. God commissioned both of us to be your spiritual companions as you journey through life. We do our best to see that evil forces do not sway you from the path that leads to heaven.

All of us belong to God's great family: you, me, the angels, and the saints. Keep in mind, sweetheart, that I am not only your queen but your mother who loves you very much.

ଔ *People display photos of their family members. Do you have an image of Mary in your house? Talk to Mary about your desire to join her in heaven.*

Priorities

February 21

My child, some people aim for one overriding goal in life. For example, they set their hearts on being a success at work, excelling at a sport, or becoming wealthy. They pour the majority of their time and energy into that chosen endeavor. For the sake of attaining their goal, they might sacrifice their friends, money, health, family, and even morals.

It's my hope that you invest your life in loving God. If you are guided by that priority instead of a temporary earthly one, you will gain true happiness, which I set as my ultimate goal for you.

Achieving your spiritual goal involves sacrifices too. Loving God means living as he wishes and spreading his kingdom. You might have to let go of certain friends, harmful habits, some pleasures, vanity, and prejudices. You might have to swim against the current.

Pray to me to pry you free from the grip a false goal may have on you. I will help you replace it with loving God. Immerse yourself in God's love and my love for you. Then you will be empowered to strive for the only goal that matters, the only goal worthy of any sacrifice.

ᘓ *Ask Mary's help in setting your sights on God alone.*

The Presence of Evil

August 3

My child, you were born for goodness and for a better world. My eyes stream with tears whenever a tragedy rocks your country. People die and are injured from natural disasters like hurricanes, earthquakes, and wild fires. Wicked human beings snuff out innocent lives and wreak havoc in your towns and cities. These catastrophes and your personal tragedies cause you great heartache. You are devastated and numb. I understand if your faith is shaken.

Suffering was not in your heavenly Father's original plan but resulted from the evil of sin. Nothing, not even the darkest moments, can separate you from God's love or mine. Jesus conquered Satan and death and opened the door to eternal bliss for you.

Be like a fish in the ocean. While storms rage overhead and turbulent currents disturb the water, swim deep where all is calm and take shelter in my love. I will hold you close and comfort you. I will remind you that the present suffering will pass. Darkness will eventually give way to light. You can look forward to an eternity when there is no crying but only laughter.

℃ *Confide in Mary your questions about the presence of evil.*

Speaking Up

August 4

My child, following my Jesus sometimes calls for speaking up to stop what is wrong. This takes a great deal of courage, especially if you are naturally reticent. John the Baptist boldly pointed out King Herod's serious sin and was executed for it. You might be in a situation where illegal activity is taking place. The right thing to do is to report it, even if it costs your job or makes enemies. Perhaps colleagues propose engaging in something immoral. Dare to speak up and head them in the right direction. Keeping silent will abet them and ensnare you in guilt.

It may be that family members or friends need correction. If you really care about them, you will tactfully inform them that they are on the wrong track.

If you are reluctant to speak up when you should, turn to me for help. I will ask the Holy Spirit to stir within you and provide the strength to act and the wisdom to know what to say. As you speak, I will be coaching you. If you suffer ill consequences, they were worth it. Your conscience will be quiet, and I will be proud of you, dear.

ଓ *Talk to Mary about circumstances where your voice could make a difference.*

Our Lady of the Snows
Dedication of the Basilica of St. Mary Major

August 5

My child, every year on this day white rose petals fall from the ceiling of the Basilica of St. Mary Major like snow in honor of the legend of the miraculous snow that indicated the site for this church. I'm touched by the way my children show their love for me. Your acts of devotion please me too. As a child, Jesus brought me flowers he picked from the fields. I like it when you present me with bouquets, placing them before my image. It also makes me glad when you perform little sacrifices in my honor, like going to Mass on a Saturday morning if possible or forgoing dessert.

Because I love you, I enjoy your company and cherish the time you spend speaking to me with prayers like the Hail Mary and the Rosary and even singing to me. What pleases me most, dear, are your efforts to imitate me, for then I know that you are growing holier.

People are glad to hear their mother praised and honored. Likewise, the love and honor you bestow on me gives joy to Jesus. If I know my son, he will bless you for this abundantly.

 Tell Mary how much you appreciate her love and help. Plan to do something in her honor.

Wounds

August 6

My child, you bear wounds from hurtful experiences you lived through, such as broken relationships, bullying, and failures. Some wounds are only scars now and indelibly mark who you are and remind you of sad times. Other wounds are fresh and haven't healed yet. It grieves me that you have suffered. I wish I could have spared you.

Jesus, too, has a wounded body, even now that he is risen and glorified. Dark red scars mark his hands, feet, and side. These wounds of Jesus are badges of victory because through them he overcame evil and won eternal life for you.

Whenever you reflect on past hurts, you still feel a twinge of pain. Sweetheart, I can't remove that memory from you as I'd like to, but I can tell you how to make your wounds meaningful. Unite them to the wounds of Jesus and offer them for the salvation of the world. No doubt, in the future more pain will be inflicted on you. Each time, endure it patiently and turn it into something fruitful. Know that I will be with you as lovingly and steadfastly as I was with Jesus throughout his ordeal. My compassionate arms will be upholding you.

ᚦ *Talk with Mary about a particular wound that bothers you.*

Your Inner Self

August 7

My child, people have different perceptions of you. Sometimes you shield yourself under a mask, so others don't know the real you. In fact, you don't always know your true self and fool yourself by thinking you do. You suppress aspects of yourself. In the center of your being you exist as you really are, which is how I see you. I know your ulterior motives, likes and dislikes, hopes, virtues, and faults.

I invite you today to sink deeply into yourself and meet the real you. Together let's take an honest look at who you are. Don't be afraid. Hold my hand and reflect on yourself answering questions like these: What gives you pleasure? What are you afraid of? What are your strengths? What are your weaknesses? What do you want in life? What matters most to you? What energizes you?

Accept yourself. You do not have to be anyone different. You do not have to try to fit in with others or meet up to their expectations. You are a beautiful and valuable person with distinctive qualities. Moreover, you are the apple of my eye. Discovering yourself brings the freedom and peace I wish you to enjoy, my darling.

૱ *Converse with Mary about discoveries you make about yourself.*

Focus

August 8

My child, at times the world is frightening and confusing. Your personal life might be pockmarked with problems and hardships. Some people escape by drink, drugs, gambling, shopping, and other distractions. Those are futile solutions that don't lead to happiness. I long to bring deep-down peace to your heart. Realize that God is in control although you don't always comprehend what he is doing. Remember that Jesus said, "I have conquered the world."[45] Because of his death and resurrection, a future of untold bliss awaits you.

In the meantime, keep your eyes fixed on God. Trust him completely to care for you with unflagging devotion as a loving father cares for his children. Also turn your gaze to me, your loving mother. Release your concerns into my compassionate hands. Depend on me to be with you, enfolding you in my arms and enabling you to weather any storms with a heart full of hope. Take the long view I have. During trials, stand firm and be patient, knowing that even the long-lasting ones are temporary.

℞ *Tell Mary that you trust her to be your unfailing support in desperate times.*

---

[45] John 16:33

Aiming High

August 9

My child, dream big and set high goals for yourself. Don't be complacent. Pursue challenging tasks instead of settling for mediocrity. You have within you the potential to do what at first seems impossible. Interview for a better job. Plan a trip to a foreign country. Decide to put an end to an addiction. Your journey up a steep mountain begins with a single step. Even if you don't quite reach the top, you still have the satisfaction of having tried, and you achieve more than before.

As you embark on your ambitious undertaking, don't think for a minute about falling. You have inner reserves you can tap in order to go beyond what you think you are capable of. Use them. Stretch yourself. Remember that one powerful and dependable tool you have at your disposal is my loving presence. Daily I urge you on to be the most you can be and do the most you can do. I will approach your heavenly Father and ask him to bless your undertaking. So don't allow fear or lack of confidence to paralyze you. Move, my darling.

cx *Talk to Mary about how you can improve your life by aiming for a daunting goal.*

Blessing Others

August 10

My child, the Spirit of Jesus dwells within you. I'd like to teach you a way to let the peace and love of this Spirit flow out from you to others. To bless someone is to call down God's favor on him or her. Whenever you encounter a person, mentally bless him or her. You might smile as you do so. Whether you engage in conversation with people or simply pass them on the street, think, "God bless you."

Bless your family members and friends this quiet way as well as people you don't exactly like. This small, hidden act of good will toward people can impact their lives in ways you'll never know and ultimately change the world. It can also change you.

When you are blessing others, you yourself will be blessed with peace and happiness. Go through this day bestowing mental blessings. See what a difference it will make in your life. By the way, sweetheart, I am continually blessing you. You are never out of my sight. If you could behold me, you would see that I am smiling at you.

ଔ *Ask Mary to help you develop the habit of mentally giving blessings.*

Expecting Jesus

August 11

My child, Jesus sometimes comes as we least expect. Who would imagine that he would first appear in the world as the child of a Jewish carpenter and his young wife? Who would think that the Son of God would play the servant, feeding people and washing feet? Jesus has a habit of surprising us. He comes to you in unexpected ways too. A supernatural vision is needed to recognize him. I, who know my son better than anyone on earth, will be glad to help you.

Today Jesus comes to you in the beggar at your door, in your sick neighbor, and in a belligerent child. He come to you in plans that go awry, in disappointments, and in calamities. Be watching for him and listen to what he is saying to you. Open yourself to the graces he offers you hidden in the encounter.

Be ready too for the second coming of my son to earth. That too will be unexpected. Don't be afraid, for it will herald the beginning of the everlasting day when, if you welcomed Jesus in your lifetime, you and I will be together forever.

ભ *Talk to Mary about past times when Jesus entered your life in unexpected ways.*

Planning with God

August 12

My child, sometimes as you carry out your plans, you meet up with one or more problems. Stymied and frustrated, you might feel like quitting. Some problems may be unavoidable—God-planted and intended to make you a stronger person. On the other hand, difficulties could arise because you neglected to consult God as you planned!

My motherly advice to you is to talk to God as you work out your activities. I was in constant communication with God as I raised his son. Divine guidance preserved me from making mistakes, and it can assist you too.

Before determining a course of action, pray to the Holy Spirit for inspiration. Ask for the grace of wisdom to do what is right and beneficial for you and others. Turn to me too for help, and I will be your advocate as you make your plans. Then as you carry them out, stay in touch with us. When you take advantage of our supernatural assistance, more than likely the path before you will be smooth and free of rocks.

ભ *Ask Mary to prompt you to ask for God's help as you plan your life.*

Love for Sinners
Our Lady, Refuge of Sinners

August 13

My child, you call me refuge of sinners, and that is what I am, a safe haven, a protection for you and others after you have offended your heavenly Father. Because I cooperated with God's plan, all sin was atoned for, repairing the original rift between the human race and God and enabling you to live with God forever. Now that I am in heaven, I'm not enjoying eternal rest. No, I'm busy responding to your request in the Hail Mary: "Pray for us sinners." I love you and all of my children no less when they sin, just as mothers on earth still love their children after they misbehave.

No sin is grievous enough that it erects an unassailable wall between you and me. I will never abandon you, but will pray with all my heart that you make things right between you and God again. I, who spent hours patching clothing, also excel at patching relationships.

I also hope that you, like me, show concern for sinners and trust that they are worthy of a second chance. I assure you that Jesus loves sinners as much as I do. After all, he gave his life for their sake.

❧ *Assure Mary that you are grateful for her prayers.*

Small Efforts

August 14

My child, you may wonder if you are making any difference in the world. Your activities seem insignificant and leave you feeling empty. Ah, I assure you that if you link your efforts to God, you will be contributing to something monumental—nothing less that the salvation of the world, dear. How do you do this?

The first thing in the morning offer God your entire day. Then as the hours pass, whenever you begin a new project, remind God that it is for him. If you are engaged in an activity that doesn't require much thought, such as mopping a floor, painting a wall, or traveling, make the time you spend more valuable by conversing with God and me.

By offering your life to God, you allow him to use you like a brush as he creates his masterpiece. That is what I did, and I never regretted it. My surrender helped accomplish the salvation of the world. In addition, it led to my becoming your mother, for which I am eternally grateful.

ငဒ *Which activities today would you want to offer God in particular? Ask Mary to remind you to do so.*

A Mother in Heaven
Assumption

August 15

My child, when my time on earth was over, because I'm the Mother of God, I went straight to heaven body and soul. I didn't have to wait until the end of the world. Now I have a glorified body like my son's when he rose from the dead. It is impossible to describe this. But I can tell you that I'm able to pass through matter and travel anywhere in the blink of an eye. I shine with radiant beauty. The wrinkles on my face and the callouses on my hands have vanished. The most wonderful thing for me about being in God's kingdom is that I am with my son.

As a child of God, you are an heir to heaven. I'm eagerly looking forward to the time when you, dear, will join us there. While on earth, if you stay close to me and Jesus and live with love as we did, someday you too will be glorified. On that day you will be able to gaze into my eyes and read there the love I have for you. That love compels me to be your constant companion, walking with you day after day and protecting you from evil until we are forever united.

ରୋ *Talk to Mary about why you look forward to heaven.*

Community

August 16

My child, what a blessing you have in belonging to the Christian community! I rejoiced at your baptism when you became a member. On that day, the Spirit laid hold of you and enflamed you with gifts. It reminded me of the time long ago when the infant Church was filled with the Spirit. I was there. When the first disciples ventured out on mission, they supported one another in the face of persecution.

You share with the community of believers a commitment to my son. Whenever you gather, the risen Lord is with you. I am too. As you pray and worship together, your faith increases and you gain strength to go out and spread the good news of the Gospel. You are equipped to add to the goodness and love in the world.

Take advantage of every golden opportunity to deepen your bonds with other followers of Jesus. This will enrich your life and theirs, and all of my children will benefit. I will look for you at the next Sunday Mass. I am praying that you are not missing or on the fringe of the group, but a vibrant worshipper at the center.

ભ *Reflect with Mary on your role in the community of believers.*

Apparitions
Our Lady of Knock

August 17

My child, you are aware of numerous reports of my appearances on earth. Some of these reports are hoaxes. On some occasions, however, I actually did visit earth because I was worried about my children. What you can be absolutely certain of is my maternal concern for you—even if you never see me with your physical eyes in this world.

When you are sad or in distress, I desire to comfort you, to embrace you in my loving arms, kiss your brow, and wipe away your tears. When you are confused and don't know what to do, I want to share with you the wisdom I possess from the long view. When you need special assistance, especially during times of temptation, I am ready to beg for graces for you.

My paramount dream for you is that you grow closer to my son every day. When you know and love my Jesus, you will be compelled to follow his teachings. You will also become more like him. I once brought Jesus to earth in Bethlehem. Now let me bring you to him in heaven. That would make me very happy.

ଔ *Tell Mary of your longing to grow closer to Jesus and ask her to help you.*

Taking Stock

August 18

My child, if you look back over your life, you'll see a mixture of deeds. You've done some good things you can be proud of and some bad things you regret. Those moments will not return. You don't get a second chance. Perhaps you haven't allowed me to assume an important role in your life. If so, that is something I sincerely hope you would rectify, dear.

Today let's peer into the future. What would you like the remaining years of your life to be like? Naturally, you hope they will be happy and peaceful. I will be with you to help your future unfurl that way. What do you need to ensure your happiness? What would you like to do before you die? What would you like to have happen? Ask me to work for you so that your hopes become a reality. I have your heavenly Father's ear in a way that no one else does.

Take my hand and let's walk together throughout the rest of your life. Know that I will be pulling for you every step of the way. You see, darling, nothing will ever quench my love for you.

ଔ *Talk to Mary about your plans for a bright future.*

Choose Joy

August 19

My child, no matter what terrible circumstances plague you, no matter how many problems confront you, your attitude is completely in your hands. You can decide to be lighthearted instead of miserable. You can choose joy. Let me give you some reasons why joy can exist within you like a calm, deep pool that nothing will disturb.

You are inundated with blessings, including your very life. Myriad family and friends love you. A beautiful and awesome creation surrounds you. That is not all. Our good God has placed you under my care. You have a heavenly mother whose unfailing love wraps around you like a warm blanket, comforting you and keeping you safe.

You can trust that God has your life mapped out and will squeeze good out of every misfortune. Don't let anything or anyone shake your trust in your heavenly Father's love for you. Ride through any storm with a smile on your face, and you will not grow old before your time. Even better, by radiating joy like the sun, you will bring joy to birth in the hearts of others.

ॐ *Tell Mary how she has brought joy to you.*

Excuses

August 20

My child, beware of making excuses for not living as a disciple of Jesus. It's easy to miss Mass because of a slight headache, to forgo volunteering for a job because you are too old or too young, or to refuse doing an act of charity because you are swamped with work. Imagine if when the Angel Gabriel came to me I excused myself from God's offer by explaining, "I'm too young," "Other girls would be better choices," or "I couldn't do that to Joseph." Then I wouldn't be the mother of Jesus or your mother.

It's also easy to excuse your faults and bad behavior. You rationalize that they are not so damaging and even trick yourself into thinking that evil is good. You attribute your failings to an inherited trait, or you blame someone for pressuring you.

When you make empty excuses, you only fool yourself. You are not being who you want to be, who God made you to be, and so you feel hollow. The antidote to excuses is prayer. Pray to the Holy Spirit, ponder God's word, and appeal to me to help you view yourself honestly. I want you to be the best version of yourself, for then you will be truly happy, darling.

ᖇ *Talk to Mary about times you offered flimsy excuses.*

An Open Mind

August 21

My child, much damage can be caused when people stubbornly cling to their own opinions. They block their progress to the truth, not to mention they make enemies. Because I want you to reach your full potential, dear, I encourage you to have a mind open to ideas that clash with yours. That means listening attentively when a person explains a view that differs from yours. You might realize that you are dead wrong about something or at least expand your knowledge about an issue.

My son had a difficult time getting through to our religious leaders because they were set in their ways. If only they had listened to him! I'd like to spare you from making their mistake. Be smarter than they were. Be willing to change your mind based on others' input.

The closer you are to the real truth, the complete truth, the closer you are to Jesus, who called himself the Truth. Think about that. Allow others to help you put the puzzle pieces of truth together. Let me help you.

ℛ *Are you wedded to the side of an issue that others challenge? Tell Mary about it.*

My Queen, My Mother
Queenship of Mary

August 22

My child, I am queen because my son is king of the universe and because I am full of grace. It gives me pleasure to reign over all creatures in heaven and on earth because it means that all of them, including you, are in my loving care. I devote myself wholeheartedly to promoting your physical and spiritual well-being.

The Old Testament recounts how Queen Esther was a powerful intercessor for her people. She risked her life asking the Persian King Ahasuerus to prevent the slaughter of her people, the Jews. I like to be called upon as an intercessor for you at the throne of Jesus.

When you have a special need, don't ever hesitate coming to me to plead your cause for you. I may be Queen Mary and Mother of God, but I am proud to be your mother too. It delights me to approach Jesus with your requests, to see the love for me glowing in his eyes, and to hear him say, "Yes, Mother." Then the worries and concerns that weigh down your heart will evaporate, and you will laugh again.

ଔ *Talk to Mary about ways you can honor her as queen. Pray the Hail, Holy Queen or the Queen of Heaven prayer.*

Saying No

August 23

My, child, you are responsible for yourself, and for the most part your life is in your hands. You must protect yourself so that you flourish both in body and soul. Sometimes this involves saying no. When someone asks you to undertake a project or a job that would add extreme pressure to your life, politely decline. Don't worry if by doing that you sink in people's estimation. You are merely doing your duty, and you will rise in my estimation.

It goes without saying that when someone tries to persuade you to do something wrong, say no. You might lose friends or become unpopular, but you will be free from guilt and shame and win my motherly approval.

There are times to say no to yourself, as when you are tempted to break a resolution, indulge in a bad habit, lash out in anger, or succumb to self-pity.

Saying no in all of these cases is how you say yes to God, and all eternity hangs on your yeses. I will help you give the responses that promote life. Just listen to my advice and you will be safe.

ଔ *Ask Mary to be with you today as you face opportunities to reply no.*

Compassion for the Hurting

August 24

My child, no one escapes suffering. Look around and be sensitive to those who are undergoing some ordeal. They may be coping with a physical challenge like a disability or a disease. They may be enduring a heartache like the death of a loved, the breakup of a relationship, or a natural disaster. And many people live in dire poverty.

My Jesus taught you to reach out to people struggling with misfortune. You might feel helpless in the face of their suffering and wonder if your efforts have any effect. I reassure you that consoling people by paying attention to them and showing that you care, is important. Recall how when Jesus was on the way to Calvary, Veronica darted out from the crowd and wiped his face with her veil. That was a small gesture but much appreciated by Jesus and by me. May you extend similar mercy to others either personally or by supporting organizations that care for them.

Know that when you suffer, I am always here ready to offer compassion to you—personally. I will hold you close to my heart beating with love for you.

ભ *Do you know someone who is suffering? Ask Mary to pray that you have the grace to ease his or her pain.*

Being an Original

August 25

My child, at times you might sense that you are different from other people, that you don't fit in with the group. Don't let that disturb you, and especially don't try to change in order to be like everyone else. You are a unique individual with your own gifts, feelings, and thoughts. Love yourself for who you are. I do, dear.

If people criticize you for being different, refer to you as "weird," or shun you, they are not real friends. Don't allow them to prevent you from being your own person. Be who you want to be. When you surrender your independence and imitate other people, you are being false to yourself and insult the God who fashioned you to be you. It will not lead to happiness.

By acknowledging that you are splashed with rich blessings and walk this earth as a one-of-a kind creation, you will grow in confidence and attain an inner joy. So be happy in your own skin, darling, and know that you do not have to go along with the crowd. Jesus and I didn't always fit in either.

ᘓ *Share with Mary what you like about yourself.*

Compromise

August 26

My child, in the near future, you are likely to be entangled in a situation where your plan is threatened by one or more persons who disagree with you. For example, you might want to spend Sunday at the beach, but a family member or friend might wish to visit a relative. Don't let an objection to your intention anger and frustrate you. To stay calm, think of me looking at you with love. Holding fast to your proposal can create hurt feelings. For your own good, dear, I suggest that you compromise. That is a key tool for keeping peace.

When you are at odds with another person about how something should be done, talk it out. Listen carefully to the other person's ideas. Together seek the middle ground. This means you must be willing to bend a little. Many times I saw palm trees in Nazareth bow almost to the ground when blasted by the hot desert winds. By being flexible they did not break. You might discover that the final decision you arrive at outshines any of the original plans. You and I will both be pleased.

ભ *Ask Mary to pray that you have the grace to be flexible not obstinate when someone opposes your plan.*

Happy Occasions
Seven Joys of Mary

August 27

My child, you may be familiar with my seven sorrows, but do you know that I also was blessed with seven great joys? They were the annunciation, the nativity of Jesus, the adoration of the Magi, the resurrection of Jesus, the ascension of Jesus, Pentecost, and my coronation as Queen of Heaven. Of course, I had more joys than these, for example, my wedding day and hearing my son speak in the synagogue for the first time.

You've had your share of sorrows, but you also experienced joys. Your baptism when you became God's child is one of them. That was a joy for me too!

Each night before you go to bed, why not reflect back on your day with me and pinpoint special blessings you experienced? Then let's thank our gracious God for his goodness to you. You can anticipate more joyful events occurring in the future. I will help make sure of that, dear. So if you are struggling now with some adversity, take heart! Remember, you were made for joy, in fact, never-ending joy.

cx *Think of seven of your major joys. Talk to Mary about them.*

In Times of Sickness
Our Lady, Health of the Sick

August 28
Saturday before the last Sunday in August

My child, I'm called health of the sick for good reasons. When the human race suffered from original sin, I helped heal that disease by cooperating with God's plan for salvation. Through praying to me, numerous people have experienced physical or spiritual healing. As your mother, I want you to be healthy and happy during your time on earth. When you are not, I am very concerned and long to make you better.

Turn to me when you are sick, in pain, facing surgery, or when death approaches. I will draw you close to my son, the Divine Physician, who gave sight to the blind and hearing to the deaf, healed the paralyzed and lepers, and restored the dead to life.

If relief from your suffering doesn't come, I will help you bear it with patience and courage. I will also inspire you to unite it with the redemptive suffering of Jesus. That way it will benefit others in our family. You have only to ask me and I will pray that you soon feel God's healing hand at work.

☙ *Talk to Mary about suffering you or a loved one may be enduring. Ask her to bring relief.*

Reconciliation

August 29

My child, misunderstandings and mistakes can shatter even the strongest relationships. When this occurs, no matter whose fault it is, your heart is wrenched and you have the bitter taste of regret in your mouth. Do not be content to leave things as they are. Rather, be the first to make an overture to patch the damage.

If you were at fault, be humble enough to ask forgiveness. If this isn't well received, at least you know you tried. If the other person caused the division, accept an apology, but if it is lacking, do or say something anyway to smooth over the crisis. Your attempts at reconciliation may be successful, and if that is the case, you will be overjoyed and blessed. My son, who knows all about reconciliation, preached, "Blessed are the peacemakers, for they will be called children of God."[46]

I understand how painful it is to approach someone to mend a relationship. It requires courage and love. Count on me to back you up and cheer you on. Both you and the one you attempt to make peace with are my beloved children.

૨ઠ *Talk to Mary about any relationship that is in need of repair.*

---

[46] Matthew 5:8

Relapses

August 30

My child, you find it depressing when you break a promise to yourself and backslide. Maybe you are determined to keep a tight rein on your temper, but then explode at your coworker or family member. Maybe you resolve to give up sweets for Lent, but then can't resist a chocolate candy bar. Maybe you aim to get up early every morning to pray, but then you give in to sleep more often than you'd like.

You have my sympathy, dear one. You and I know that you have several admirable qualities, but you are not perfect. You can expect a few falls. There's no need to beat yourself up over a relapse. Just forgive yourself and start over again. You might have to start over dozens of times!

Each time you begin anew to keep a resolution, you become stronger. Let this be crystal clear: you are not alone as you aim to be your very best self. I am with you every step of the way, hoping and praying for your ultimate success.

ℭ *Tell Mary about a resolution you would like to keep and ask her help.*

Things Undone

August 28

My child, when you have a mountain of things to do, you do not always accomplish all of them. Don't be distressed, but accept the fact that you are human and limited. You can't work miracles. It could be that you were not meant to do the tasks left undone at that particular time. Possibly you will be able to work on them later and more successfully when you are not under a lot of pressure. Maybe you were not supposed to undertake certain tasks at all, but leave them for others to do.

Of course, if your workload is unfinished because you have been shirking, that is another matter. Wasting time in leisure activities or procrastinating when duty calls only hurts you in the end. When you feel lethargic and inclined to ignore your responsibilities, ask me to light a fire under you.

I carried out all of my daily chores for love of Jesus and Joseph. I suggest that you offer your work for an intention close to your heart, perhaps for the benefit of one of your loved ones. Then your labor will be sheer joy.

 C₰ *Prioritize the items on your to do list. Ask Mary to help you accomplish the major ones and not worry if you don't get around to the rest.*

September

Irritating People

September 1

My child, no doubt you come across a few people whose habits irritate you. They might even be family members. You would like to avoid them so they don't ruin your day. There is the woman who brags about her family, the girl who talks incessantly, the man who never has anything good to say about anything. Then there's the one who is always right and makes you feel as though you know nothing. To be honest, when I approached the well and saw a certain neighbor there, I was tempted to turn around and fetch water later.

Changing annoying people is hopeless, so don't even try. You can, however, control your reaction to them, dear. In their presence, stay calm. Do your best to form a positive attitude to these difficult people. They are God's children too, and they might be carrying burdens that would bring tears to your eyes if you knew about them.

Jesus did not ask you to like everyone. That is impossible. But you are to love them as I do, that is, to wish them well. Viewing them through my compassionate eyes will help you tolerate their faults.

ल *Speak to Mary about people who rub you the wrong way.*

Accepting Help

September 2

My child, God places people in your life who will help you. They channel his love for you. How grateful I was that God sent Joseph to me as a helpmate and later, when I was a childless widow, the apostle John! As Jesus carried the cross, he was given Simon of Cyrene's help.

Your strong streak of independence and pride make you reluctant to admit you could use help. Therefore, you decline people's offer to carry a load, cook a meal for you, or take you somewhere. You say, "No, thank you" or "I can manage." You remind me of Peter who said to Jesus, "You will never wash my feet."[47] The next time someone offers to lend you a hand, I will tap you on the shoulder and say, "Accept their help."

When you reject people's offer of help or refuse to ask them to do you a favor, you deny them the chance to perform a good deed. You deprive them of the warm, satisfying feeling that results from helping someone. You also block God's love that flows to you through them.

Along with asking others for help, don't forget to ask me. I am always eager to assist you.

ଶ *Talk to Mary about where you could use someone's help. Ask her to pray that you have the humility to accept it.*

---

[47] John 13:8

Good Shepherds
Mother of the Divine Shepherd

September 3

My child, you probably have not met many shepherds. In our day, they and their flocks were a constant sight on our hills. Remember that shepherds were the first to hear the good news of Jesus' birth. My son called himself a good shepherd, meaning that he cared for his followers to the point of sacrificing his life for them.

As the mother of Jesus, I was the shepherd of this Good Shepherd for most of his life, preparing his meals, making his clothes, and keeping him from harm. I, your heavenly mother, will shepherd you throughout your life too, sweetheart.

I will gently prod you to stay on the right path, and I will fend off the Evil One when he tries to attack you. As you sleep, I will watch over you. To nourish your spiritual life, I will lead you the Eucharist, where you will be fed with sacred bread and wine. Held tightly in my loving arms, you will always be safe and secure. While others may fret about the future, you never need to worry or be afraid of anything. I will always be looking out for you with steadfast love.

ᘓ *Read Psalm 23, the Good Shepherd psalm, and talk to Mary about it.*

Comfort in Time of Trouble
Our Lady of Consolation

September 4

My child, I love being called the comfort of the afflicted. When life weighs heavily on you or when unexpected tragedy strikes and you are devastated, know that I care deeply about you and long to ease your pain. Whenever Jesus would get hurt as a boy, I soothed him by holding him in my arms and kissing him. When he was injured in the workshop, I doctored him. When people cheated him or made fun of him, my reassuring words calmed him. I only wish I could have comforted him when he wept over Jerusalem and when his friend Lazarus died.

I am always ready and eager to console you, my beloved child, in times of sadness, doubt, or confusion. When you are hurting, I hurt too and yearn to dispel your distress. Come to me so I can enfold you in my ever-compassionate arms close to my heart and whisper words of comfort. I will reassure you that you are not alone and are very precious to me. Let the knowledge of my love and the profound love of your heavenly Father be a healing balm to you.

છ *Talk to Mary about anything that is upsetting you.*

The Real You

September 5

My child, on days when you are tired, troubled by a failure, or in a tizzy, you tend to think ill of yourself. A nagging voice inside you says negative things like, "You can't do anything right," "There you go again," and "If people knew what you were really like, they wouldn't like you." Dear, hush that voice and stop being so hard on yourself. You have a distorted picture of yourself quite different from the way I see you.

You are a wonderful person, and I think the world of you. So does God. Didn't Jesus say that your heavenly Father has the hairs on your head counted and you are of more value than many sparrows?[48]

As for your mistakes, I certainly don't condemn you for them. You are a saint in the making. Naturally you make missteps. With my loving support, you will continue to become what you wish to be as you take the high road to holiness. Banish any toxic thoughts, those lies about you, and replace them with uplifting and encouraging thoughts about yourself. I will help you.

ભ *Talk to Mary about developing a realistic picture of yourself.*

---

[48] Matthew 10:31

Be Salt

September 6

My child, Jesus said, "You are the salt of the earth."[49] He meant you. I used salt from the Dead Sea for two reasons. As a preservative, it kept the fish we ate from decaying. I also added salt to food to bring out the flavor.

By saying you are salt, Jesus implied that you are to save the world from decadence and corruption. You do that by spreading his teachings, which promote goodness, and by working to halt evil activities. Whenever you overcome your hesitancy and speak boldly about Christ, you are salt. Whenever you stick out your neck and warn someone that they are endangering their immortal soul, you are salt. Whenever you support people and legislation that favor justice and peace, you are salt.

You are also to be salt by drawing goodness and sweetness out of other people. Point out their good points and encourage them to be their best selves. Sometimes you can influence others merely by the force of your good example. Count on that having a ripple effect.

I was excellent salt on earth and still am. Look to me for assistance as you make the earth a better place.

℞ *Talk to Mary about some way you can foster goodness.*

---

[49] Matthew 5:13

Lack of Love

September 7

My child, one of the most painful things is to be unloved. A great deal of misery stems from feeling all alone. You can be the wealthiest, the most successful, or the most famous person, and yet be unhappy when love is missing from your life. Don't be afraid that no one will cherish you as beloved. You will never lack love because my love for you is everlasting. No matter what you do, even if you commit the gravest sin, I will never abandon you, dear one.

In all of your joys and sorrows, I am with you, holding you close to my heart. I hear every word you say and see everything you do. You may not be aware of me, but I am always present to you. During frightening stretches of your life, you have only to turn to me and I will be your sturdy support. When you have a special request, I will gladly intercede for you before our heavenly Father. Are you worried about something? Let my love for you dissolve your concerns.

Allow the knowledge of my deep love for you to sink into your mind and heart. Rejoice in my love.

↷ *Tell Mary about your love for her.*

Gift of Life
Nativity of the Blessed Virgin Mary

September 8

My child, I know my birth thrilled my parents, Joachim and Anne. I imagine that when I was finally born, in heaven the angels and the saints, especially Adam and Eve, clapped for joy. They knew that salvation for the human race was on the horizon. No one other than my son has ever meant so much to the world and to you as I do. Thank God with me for the beautiful gift of my life.

From all eternity, our heavenly Father planned my birth, but he also planned yours. On the day you were born, I rejoiced and gave thanks. You were another person destined to share God's life and glorify him forever. The purpose of my life, what I was born for, was not only to be God's mother but to be your mother who cares for and cherishes you. Wherever your journey on earth takes you and no matter how long it lasts, I will be with you.

I only wish one gift from you on my birthday, and that is nothing less than your heart. You already have mine, dear child.

ଔ *Tell Mary what she means to you.*

Uncharted Territory

September 9

My child, each morning as you open your eyes, you face uncharted territory. You don't know whom or what you will encounter that day. You will forge new paths for yourself, all the time trying to be the best version of yourself you can muster in any circumstances. Along the way you may meet friends, enemies, treacherous rivers, a wilderness, sunny meadows, and perhaps a storm or two.

I, your devoted mother, am happy to serve as your companion and guide. With me at your side you will be surefooted and lighthearted. Consult me when you lose your way, are crossing rough terrain, or are threatened by hostile creatures. I will be a reliable partner, coaching you, alerting you to danger, and protecting you. When you trip, I will catch you.

At night as you climb into bed, you will realize that your day's journey has either been a pleasant one or you have managed with my help to overcome any problems. You will be able to close your eyes in peace and expect sweet dreams. Imagine me covering you with my love as with a soft, cozy blanket.

ଔ *Tell Mary how you will depend on her tomorrow.*

A Visit

September 10

My child, break away from the whirlwind of activities that surround you and sit quietly with me. Leave your pressures, your stresses, and worries behind. Take a deep breath and relax. Just enjoy my company. I always look forward to our time together.

Speak to me in words others composed that express what is in your heart. Or just talk to me spontaneously. Tell me whatever you wish. I'm interested in every facet of your life. What is going on in your life and in the world and how do you feel about it? Share with me your hopes and dreams as well as anything you want to get off your chest. Don't be concerned that you will say something you shouldn't. Nothing can surprise me or make me think any less of you. You can be totally yourself with me, my darling.

Then listen in silence to me. Hear me assure you of my love and gently suggest that you spend more time talking with my son. He also loves it immensely when you focus on him. Both of us eagerly anticipate the day when you are born into eternal life never to leave our presence.

ଦ *Spend some time talking to Mary right now about anything on your mind.*

Struggles

September 11

My child, during life you periodically engage in battles. Enter the fray with courage. As you strive to conquer whatever you are fighting, whether it is an unjust system, a serious disease, a personal fault, or the wiles of the devil, don't get discouraged or quit. It would be foolish to surrender. Rather, when you are flagging, throw yourself into my arms. I will pray that you receive strength in your weakness and even do battle for you. Trust me to work on your behalf.

Enduring your trials successfully can yield outcomes beyond your wildest dreams. Stay resolute and be patient. Good things sometimes take a long time to blossom. Have faith. Even if you don't emerge victorious, your struggles are opportunities for growth. Remember that God is for you and so am I. Your heavenly Father has carefully plotted out your life and has prepared a place for you free from strife. Each of your victories brings you closer to that place and to me. Eventually you will enjoy everlasting peace.

ଔ *Are you in the midst of a particular struggle right now? Ask Mary to help.*

The Power of a Name
The Holy Name of Mary

September 12

My child, it's said that the sweetest sound to us is someone saying our name. My heart rejoices when I hear you calling me by name. Of my more than two thousand titles, my favorite way to be addressed is simply "Mary." The Hebrew form of my name, Miryam, means "bitter," which is apt considering the hardships my life entailed. Do you know what your name means?

Names represent people. That is why my name is holy. So is my son's. In fact, Scripture says that at the name of Jesus every knee should bend.[50] Every person's name ought to be handled with care.

When people honor my name—for instance, by naming people or things for me—they honor me. Names have power. Pronouncing my name draws me to you like a magnet. Say my name often, even a hundred times a day, and say it with great love. That is how I will say your name when we meet face-to-face. I will greet you ecstatically with my arms extended and a radiant smile.

ℂ *Talk to Mary about her name and yours.*

---

[50] Philippians 2:10

An Inflated Self-Image

September 13

My child, you are capable of wondrous things. However, sometimes you are disheartened because you aren't able to accomplish your goals. Maybe despite your best efforts, your errant child is incorrigible, your financial problems remain, the candidate you campaigned for loses, and certain relationships are still strained. You may think you can solve all of your problems, your friends' problems, and some of the world's problems; but reality tells you otherwise.

I remind you that you are not the Messiah. You can't work miracles and fix everything. Actually, God doesn't expect you to. But I am the mother of the Messiah and have access to unlimited power. Feel free to appeal to me for assistance whenever your heart is set on a certain intention. With my backing, your chances of succeeding multiply. You are very important to me, dear, and I will be happy to make your wishes mine. If our requests are not granted, you can assume that our good and gracious Lord, who loves both of us more than we will ever know, has good reasons.

ଔ *Share with Mary the intentions uppermost in your mind.*

The Cross, Our Hope

September 14

My child, I don't know how I could bear standing at the cross and watching Jesus die such an agonizing death. No mother should have to go through something like that. However, three days later, my son appeared to me glorified. You can imagine the exhilaration I felt when he spoke to me alive and well. Jesus achieved your salvation, and now it is up to you to do your part.

You are responsible for living so that the grace of God shines out from you. You must do the work of God and have the nerve to confront the powers of evil and sin. This is a tall order, my darling, but you will be equipped for it if you rely on my help. I will sustain you and coax you to persevere.

One piece of advice is to accept crosses that mark your path and unite them with my son's. Don't worry. Just as love compelled me to accompany Jesus on his journey of suffering, it makes me be faithful to you during hard times. Then at the end of your road, you too will rise in glory. You have my son's word.

ଊ *Tell Mary you appreciate the sacrifice she and her son made so that you might live.*

The Fires of Pain
Seven Sorrows of the Blessed Virgin Mary

September 15

My child, sorrows in life are inevitable. Being God's mother did not spare me from them either. My sorrows flowed from events in my son's life, mainly the conflict Jesus faced, fleeing into Egypt to save his life, losing Jesus in Jerusalem, meeting him on the way to Calvary, the crucifixion, taking him down from the cross, and his burial. The sorrows Simeon foretold were like seven swords piercing my heart.

So you see, dear, I know what pain is. I understand when you are overcome with sorrow, and my heart aches for you. Has a loved one died? Have you failed at something? Are you sick physically or mentally? Have you been betrayed? At such times, please realize that I, your mother, wish to comfort you and douse the pain that sears your heart. I will embrace you tenderly in my compassionate arms, smooth the furrows from your brow, and dry your tears. Be aware of my constant presence and know that I am alert to your every cry and every sigh. As soon as troubles arise, confide them in me. Let wave after wave of my profound love wash over you.

Talk to Mary about something that causes you grief.

Be Not Afraid!

September 16

My child, frightening things flood your world: political and corporate corruption, drug abuse, human trafficking, violence, pollution, terrorism, and the threat of nuclear war. You have my sympathy. The age I lived in was also rife with evils. Rome occupied my country and oppressed my people. We were subjected to cruel, immoral, and incompetent leaders; and we had our share of bandits and prostitutes.

Never give up hope for a better world. You may feel overwhelmed and helpless. Your efforts to establish the reign of God may seem puny and futile. You may think you lack the time, strength, and goodness to make a difference.

When you sense that you are drowning and struggling to breathe, look to me to be your safety net. I will keep you from going under. You do not have to purify the world singlehandedly. Ask me to join you in your endeavors. As we work together, your actions to promote justice, peace, and love will gain momentum and effect changes you may not learn of until the next life. Because of my son, you can look forward with confidence to a new creation.

Talk with Mary about how you can improve a bad situation.

273

Optimism

September 17

My child, it's hard to maintain your equilibrium when one thing after another goes wrong. Equipment breaks, you make mistakes, people disappoint you, you stub your toe, or it rains the day you planned an outing. When a barrage of misfortune befalls you, you wonder if the dark days will ever end and your spirits sink. You thirst for a break in the pattern of bad luck when everything will return to normal. Come to me. I will be a refreshing oasis for you. Snug in my arms you will revive.

Open your eyes to the good things, maybe things you have overlooked in the past. I will point them out. Some are extraordinary, but you take them for granted. When you focus on your blessings, your minor irritations fade. In the great expanse of time and eternity and in the context of your entire life, they are nothing.

Cultivate a positive outlook on yourself, other people, and the world. Rise above your current setbacks and anticipate your future with high hopes. Believe me, God has a wondrous plan for you. I will be with you as your chief encourager as it plays out.

℘ *Are you in a good place in your life now or not? Talk to Mary about it.*

Near to God

September 18

My child, do you ever feel that God is far away? You don't sense his presence and wonder if he has abandoned you? God never deserts you, but perhaps you distanced yourself from him through neglect or by flouting his will. You can't really run from God. "In him we live and move and have our being."[51] Your heavenly Father is closer to you than you are to yourself, and he knows you better than you know yourself. He loves you with an infinite love and is thrilled to forgive you when you are contrite.

Finding God again is not complicated. You need not resort to strange rituals, long prayers, or extraordinary penances. Just give God the time and space to contact you. Be alert to him acting in the marvelous world around you and in subtle ways in your daily experiences.

Because I'm closer to God than any other creature, I have unalloyed bliss. I pray that you stay centered on God by speaking to him, thinking about him, and doing what pleases him. Then you too will be filled with joy. I would like that very much because I want the best for you.

ᑫ *Talk to Mary about your relationship with God and how you can strengthen it.*

---

[51] Acts 17:28

Imperfections

September 19

My child, what people think of you is difficult to change. They tend to recall their first impression of you and then keep you in that box. But you always have the ability to change and to improve. You can break out of that box and move on. You are in control of your life.

When I look at you, I see you as you are now but also as you have the potential to become. I would love to help you sculpt yourself into the person God created you to be. I have expertise in matters of the soul.

So take an honest look at yourself with me. What area needs improvement? Change doesn't usually occur overnight. We will work on it incrementally. Each day brings another opportunity to be a better you. Little by little we will perfect you, chipping here and sanding there.

When you are tempted to give up the task, rely more on me. I will call on my son, who was adept at shaping things in his woodwork shop. The three of us will collaborate in making you over so that people might not even recognize you. You will be proud of yourself.

ᘓ *Tell Mary an imperfection you would like to eliminate with her help.*

Generosity of Soul
September 20

My child, occasions arise that challenge you to be generous in hidden, spiritual ways. Someone's remark or action offends you. Instead of responding with a tongue lashing or the silent treatment, be big enough to overlook it. An opponent or a friend achieves something you desired. Swallow your envy and celebrate with him or her. You are kept waiting when a doctor or someone else is late. Resist punishing that person by pointing out the inconvenience. An acquaintance is sick or in trouble. Assist him or her anonymously by praying and doing penance. Don't be stingy with kindness. Let it flow freely.

As your day wears on, I will call your attention to opportunities for being generous. They will require you to win little victories over yourself. I will ask the Holy Spirit within you to give you the grace to react in a beautiful, large-hearted way. When you practice generosity of spirit, my Jesus, who is never outdone in kindness, will shower you with blessings. I will be aware of your secret deed, and I will be immensely proud of you, my darling.

ᔓ *Talk to Mary about ways you might love others by secretly being generous.*

Appeal to Mary

September 21

My child, some people think it is foolish to pray to me. They believe you should only pray directly to God. Sadly, they deprive themselves of a tremendous resource. I hope you understand that the way to the heart of Jesus is through me, his mother. I can influence him as no one else can. Also, Jesus thoughtfully presented me to you as your mother. He shares me with you, and so please let me be a mother to you.

My love for you is an ocean, so deep and wide you can't fathom it. I'm with you always, watching over you and waiting for you to speak to me. I am eager to have you turn over your problems to me. I will listen to your requests and beg Jesus to answer them.

When your earthly mother is no longer with you, I still will be there to advise you, protect you, and hug away your hurts. At the first sign of trouble, don't think twice about coming immediately to me. I will do my utmost to restore your peace. And Jesus will be pleased that you are taking advantage of his gift.

ൠ *Tell Mary how much you appreciate her loving care. Pray: Mother of Jesus, be mother to me.*

Be Yeast

September 22

My child, juxtaposed with the massive challenges of the world, you might consider yourself small and weak, too powerless to effect much change. Nevertheless, you have amazing potential, especially when you are coupled with me. When I made bread at home, I added yeast. Just a tiny bit transformed a whole loaf and made it rise. You, dear, can become like yeast. You have the latent ability to touch and uplift people around you. Activate it!

I'll help you foster courage to be outspoken when it comes to defanging evil and promoting good and right. Do this in little ways—by counseling family members and friends and by offering them the witness of your faithful life. On a broader scale, take action and support practices and policies that benefit others.

As you work to permeate the world with the reign of God, I will be your unfailing support, stirring you to action and cheering you on. I guarantee that you will be surprised at the widespread results, if not in this world, in the next, dear.

  ଔ *Share with Mary any doubts you have about your power to do good and enlist her help.*

If Only

September 23

My child, don't let "if onlys" paralyze you. If only I were wealthier, if only I had normal childhood, if only I had a better job, if only I weren't so young (or so old), and similar laments can be lame excuses that keep you from being honest about your poor performance. They are a net ensnaring you so that you do not achieve the life you really want and experience the full joy I hope would characterize your life.

Sometimes you can cut yourself loose from these negative factors and move on. For example, you might say, "If only my life weren't so monotonous, I'd be happier." Well, taking up a hobby, learning something new, or joining an organization would add a dollop of excitement to your life. With a little creativity, which I would be happy to supply, you could override your drawbacks. Some disadvantages are nonnegotiable, out of your control. Instead of focusing on their downside, look for something positive about them.

Don't deal with your "if onlys" alone. Call on me for help. I will guide you to see your life from my perspective, which is God's perspective. Then we will get to work.

ය *Talk to Mary about aspects of your life that hold you back*

Compassion
Our Lady of Mercy (Ransom)

September 24

My child, my son is mercy incarnate and the living sign of God's compassion on the human race. Therefore, I am literally the mother of mercy. But I am also a merciful mother. I never fail to hear the cries of my children when they are in misery, and I come to their aid. That includes you, dear.

If you are in trouble or in need of comfort, call upon me. I will hasten to your side and devote myself to helping you. I will pour out my love on you, strengthen you, and accompany you through whatever hardships or heartaches you are enduring.

When you have wounded my son by sin, I do not forsake you. After you fall, I pick you up, dust you off, and give you a hug. I forgive you and lead you back to Jesus. There I will be your advocate. Believe me, Jesus, too, is quick to forgive. I've seen him forgive people many times, most notably those apostles who deserted him after he was arrested. Both of us wish to protect you from grief on earth and, most of all, from eternal misery.

 CR *Thank Mary for being a refuge for you whenever you are hurting or in distress.*

Conversation

September 25

My child, what a joy to speak to a loved one frequently. Imagine the long conversations Jesus and I had during the thirty years he lived with me. I cherish the memory of those talks. I also treasure the time you spend talking with me, my dear. I like it when you share your troubles, heartaches, and joys. I welcome your requests for help and gladly intercede for you with Jesus.

I am easy to contact, for I am right at your elbow whether you are in your house, at work, at social events, or outside in God's beautiful world. Because you don't see me, you must make an effort to remember me. Perhaps you would form the habit of greeting me with a Hail Mary in the morning and in the evening. During the day, send me a short message every once in a while, so I know you are thinking of me.

One of the sharpest pains is not hearing from a beloved one. Spare me that pain, my darling, by staying in close communication with me. I will always listen to you with an open heart. And when you are quiet, you will hear me speak to you. Most often I will be saying, "I love you."

ಆ *Spend some quiet time conversing with Mary.*

Harmony

September 26

My child, you are engaged in making your life a beautiful melody of praise. Be vigilant that you are always in tune with God's will for you. The Evil One looks for opportunities to create discord in your song. Bad companions attempt to distract you so that you are off-key. Circumstances and hardships pressure you to quit producing lovely music altogether.

Don't be deterred from your holy pursuit that infuses your life with meaning and happiness. Fighting fatigue and discouragement, focus on it tenaciously and passionately.

Every day renew your commitment to follow God's score faithfully. Look to me as your reliable conductor who knows the music by heart. I will firmly yet gently lead you to play note by note, chord by chord in a way that harmonizes with the universe and gives glory to God. If you follow my lead, sweetheart, at the end of your life, when you take your final bow, you will hear heaven resound with the applause of the angels and saints. My clapping will be the loudest.

ભ *Talk to Mary about anything hindering you from being in harmony with God.*

Motherly Guidance
Mary, Star of the Sea

September 27

My child, at times you sail through treacherous seas and dangerous weather. When you are buffeted by storms and lost at sea, confused and frightened, have recourse to me. My title Star of the Sea invites you to do this. I love this name, for it reflects the role I am privileged to play in your life. Just as the North Star guides seafarers, I guide you and preserve you from shipwreck.

On your journey, inevitably you encounter trials and hardships. With my assistance, your boat will not capsize no matter how powerful the wind and waves. You will never go astray or drown. I help you navigate safely through perilous shoals of temptation. Shining brightly, I hover over you and illumine your path on the darkest of days. When great suffering overwhelms you, remember that only in darkness can you see the stars. In the sunshine of ordinary days, you might forget me, although I am always there.

Keep your gaze fixed on me as a bright star. I will lead you along the labyrinth of your life to the harbor of heaven, your final destination.

ଓ *Talk to Mary about problems you are dealing with currently. Sing or pray the ancient hymn "Ave Maris Stella" (Hail, Star of the Sea).*

Divine Birthright

September 28

My child, when you don't think much of yourself, I am disturbed. I remind you that because God made you in his image, you have untold dignity and splendor. Incredibly, his intention was and still is for union with you. Even now the almighty God dwells within you, making you a living sanctuary and worthy of angels' reverence. On that fateful day when I said yes to God, Jesus became human and thereby restored your potential for becoming divine. Each time you celebrate the Eucharist, you are a step closer to reclaiming your inheritance. Your body is destined to be transformed into a copy of my son's risen and glorious one.

Your task on earth is to become more Godlike, in other words, holy. Don't worry, dear, when you become acutely aware of your frailty and limitations. Let them drive you into the comfort of my arms. When you are weak, there is more space for God to act. Sustained by my aid and God's, you will become what you desire to be, what God aches for you to be and what I am today — a divinized person aglow with life and love.

☙ *Tell Mary about your thirst for holiness. Ask her to help you achieve it.*

Worship
St. Michael, St. Gabriel, and St. Raphael
September 29

My child, the main occupations of angels are worshiping and serving God. When Satan declared, "I will not serve," and desired to be worshipped himself, he was consigned to the fire of hell. You are privileged to have the same purpose as the angels. You are to glorify and serve God on earth and in heaven as I do.

You glorify God on earth when on beholding one of his marvelous works your heart leaps up and you declare, "I adore you, Lord." You praise God in prayers and call him blessed, especially during the Eucharistic celebration. You honor God when you dedicate your life to him, every moment of every day.

Resist the temptation to swerve from glorifying God and seek your own glorification instead. Sometimes you must wrestle with your ego. With my prayers to support you, child, you will be faithful in staying true to your purpose, the noblest task there is. You will join me and the angels in saying, "My soul magnifies the Lord,"[52] both here and in the next world.

૭ૐ *Talk to Mary about sights or experiences that make your heart swell with adoration.*

---

[52] Luke 1:46

Praying with God's Book

September 30

My child, you can touch God and be touched by God when you pray with his book, the Bible. Although I couldn't read Scripture, I had many of its lovely verses memorized. At appropriate times and at odd times these would come to the fore of my mind. This phenomenon made me more conscious of God's presence. I recommend that you learn some of God's words by heart.

When I heard Scripture read, often a word or phrase would strike my heart like lightning. I would repeat it over and over and ponder what meaning God had hidden in it for me. After I realized what he was saying to me and why, I burst into a response: words of love, praise, gratitude, or joy. Then my mind became still, and I simply rested in God's presence. For me, this period of contemplation was like spending time in heaven for a little while.

Dear, when you find it difficult to pray, pick up your Bible, and read a few verses until you are snagged. Then pray like I did. I know the experience will lead you to a deeper relationship with our heavenly Father.

ଔ *Tell Mary of your desire to become more familiar with God's Word. Plan how you will read it daily.*

October

Little Things

October 1

My child, you do not need to do extraordinarily difficult things to be holy. You do not have to die for the faith or preach it in foreign lands. I didn't do these things, but I obeyed God. I took care of my family and carried out my chores with love.

Offering every slight action to God suffuses them with great power and you with grace. Holiness is right at your fingertips. Every stitch you sew, every pot you stir, and every floor you sweep, brings you closer to God. Whenever you stretch out your hands to someone in need, soothe a fevered brow, or bestow a hug, you add a jewel to the crown prepared for you in heaven.

While you are about your daily business, think of me from time to time. I will remind you that when you perform your jobs well and make them a gift to God, he will rain down blessings on you. Be alert to the holiness wrapped in little things. Living a simple life and trusting in God's love will not make you world famous, but in my eyes you will be a saint.

ര *Ask Mary to help you to remember to pray the Morning Offering consciously every day.*

Guardian Angels

October 2

My child, angels are real. I live with these majestic creatures who praise and serve God. As pure spirits, angels are invisible but can assume a body. The Angel Gabriel appeared to me when I was a young girl. I was frightened, but he said, "Do not be afraid." On the night Jesus was born, an angel delivered the Good News to shepherds. The angel told them, "Do not be afraid." Then hundreds of angels joined him, praising God. You needn't be afraid either because not only do you have me to protect you but a specific angel, a personal bodyguard, is with you throughout your life.

My son confirmed this. He said that the Father has entrusted each of his children into the care of an angel.[53] Your guardian angel watches over you and prompts you to make good choices. When you are tempted, why not ask your angel to come to your aid? Remember to thank him for his care. You can look forward to meeting your angel in heaven. I will be happy to introduce you.

ભ *Talk to Mary about times to speak to your guardian angel.*

---

[53] Matthew 18:10

Care for Creation

October 3

My child, one of life's joys is being surrounded by God's magnificent creation. I loved to walk through barley fields, to sit on the shore of the Sea of Galilee, to smell the scent of rain, and to watch the antics of baby lambs and goats. You appreciate God's world, too. I've seen you savoring a glorious sunset, stopping to look at a delicate flower, and playing with a pet.

God entrusted creation into our care. I weep when people scar the land, pollute the air, poison lakes and streams, and endanger animals. An assault on God's masterpiece is an insult to him. I beg you, child, do try to counteract the damage already done to the world. Take steps to prevent further destruction.

I will help you fulfill your responsibility to be God's good steward. I'll ask the Holy Spirit to inspire you with ideas for action and to provide you with the courage and zeal needed to carry them out. God is praised in all his works. I thank you for anything you do to preserve their pristine goodness and beauty.

ख *Talk to Mary about environmental concerns that are prominent today.*

Discouragement

October 4

My child, horrible world events, your life's harsh realities, or your failures to live up to your dreams can cast a pall over you. One moment you are at peace and happy. Then without warning, your joy shrivels up, and you plod through the hours or even days engulfed by a murky atmosphere, lost and crestfallen.

At such times, darling, hear me calling your name and inviting you to take shelter in the cave of my heart. You can never plumb the depths of my motherly love for you. I look on you with understanding eyes and sympathize with you when you are downcast. I have known similar periods of distress and sorrow. I remember my fear when Herod sought to kill Jesus, my guilt when we couldn't find him for three days, and my devastation when my son was tortured and executed.

I will keep you company during the dark time. I will work incessantly, asking Jesus to relieve your sadness if it is his will, until the sun breaks through the clouds once more and you can smile again.

◌ℛ *Tell Mary that when you need comfort or encouragement, you hope you will remember to turn to her.*

Working with Mary

October 5

My child, every day you must shoulder a number of tasks. Some are monumental, daunting projects, while others are trivial jobs. No matter how complex and significant a task or how simple and mundane, you will accomplish it more successfully when you make me your partner. When Joseph or Jesus needed help in the carpenter shop I was always glad to hold a board straight or sort nails.

If you doubt that you have what it takes to do a job, turn to me for a helping hand. Even if you possess the knowledge, skill, and strength to tackle a job, the outcome will be better with my help. So before undertaking anything, send up a prayer, asking me to secure God's blessing on it. And while you are working, elicit my intercession. Every now and then shoot me a quick plea, like "Help, Mary," and I will hasten to your aid and see that things go swimmingly.

Put your heart into your work and do your best. I won't do everything for you, but you can count on my assistance.

ભ *Talk to Mary about tasks on today's agenda. Enlist her help.*

Unanswered Prayers

October 6

My child, suppose for a long time you pour out your heart in prayer for a good intention, but it seems as though God is asleep in the boat. Or you pray for one thing to happen, and the opposite occurs. For example, you pray for a little girl who is seriously ill, but she dies. Jesus promised several times, "Whatever you ask for in prayer with faith, you will receive."[54] My son doesn't lie. So why aren't your prayers answered?

You might conclude that you do not have enough faith, or that your sins build a wall between you and God. Your faith might be shaken, and you might even doubt that God exists.

God is always your attentive, loving Father. He hears your every word. His answer could be "No, in the long run that wouldn't be good" or "I have a better idea" or "Be patient." Don't neglect this powerful strategy: Call upon me to intercede for you. I will bolster your request by presenting it to God myself. If you still don't receive the answer you hope for, I will pray that you accept God's will and align your will with his. That will bring you peace.

 Entrust your intentions to Mary.

---

[54] Matthew 21:22

293

Praying for Peace
Our Lady of the Most Holy Rosary

October 7

My child, in the face of all the violence in the world, you are distressed and feel helpless. What can you possibly do to douse the flames of conflict erupting in countries and city streets? Praying the Rosary, especially as a family, is a strong, effective action to promote peace, and yet it is so simple.

As the beads slip through your fingers, you think about the life of Jesus and recite prayers, mostly Hail Marys. The Rosary is comparable to presenting me with a garland of beautiful roses. By honoring me, you honor my son, who loves me. You please both of us.

When your heart is troubled and yearns for peace, spare fifteen minutes or so to pray the Rosary. Some people pray it to fall asleep! It would make me happy if you prayed a Rosary every day, my darling. That devotion increases your intimacy with me. You stay close to me and within my embrace. I will help you to be at peace with God, with others, and with yourself. And little by little peace may reign over countries.

ᑲ *Talk to Mary about your attitudes toward the Rosary.*

Motivation

October 8

My child, let's peer into your heart to detect why you strive to do good. What motivates you to obey God and resist doing wrong? There are several possibilities. You could have been brought up that way, or you could want to maintain a good reputation. You could be afraid of being caught if you do wrong. Perhaps you desire the perfect happiness that is the reward of living a good life, or maybe you fear spending eternity in the fires of hell. You might be prompted to walk the straight and narrow for a combination of these reasons.

Let me tell you the most excellent and most compelling motivator for doing good and refraining from evil. It is loving God so fiercely that you'd rather die than do anything to displease him. I wish such love would take root in your heart, dear. That is the kind of love God has for you. It is eternal and unconditional. God doesn't love you because you are good. You do good because you experience God's love and desire to reciprocate. Love is expressed in deeds. I pray that you come to know and love our good and gracious God as I do.

ℭ℞ *Talk to Mary about evidence of God's love for you.*

295

Holy Places

October 9

My child, after Jacob dreamed of a ladder going to heaven, he exclaimed, "Surely the LORD is in this place — and I did not know it!"[55] In Nazareth for years God dwelt among my neighbors, but they didn't know it. Today I ask you, dear, to open your eyes wide to where God is. Yes, God is in churches in a special way, but he is present too in your house, your neighbor's house, the place where you work, in hospitals, in prisons, and in the hovels of the poor. He lives in everyone you meet. Your whole earth is sacred because Jesus walked its ground and breathed its air.

One amazing residence of God is your very heart. Not many people realize that — really realize it. God is ignored and kept waiting. I ask you, dear, to be conscious of God living in you, no less than he lived in me for nine months, no less than he abides in tabernacles. From time to time, sink down into the abyss of your being and meet God there. I will join you as you adore your heavenly Father and love him.

◌ℬ *Ask Mary to keep you aware of God dwelling within you.*

---

[55] Genesis 28:16

Firming Up Faith

October 10

My child, as I held the infant Jesus in my arms and he drew sustenance from me, I marveled at this mystery that I should be feeding God. It was incredible. I'm sure there are days when you find it hard to believe that almighty God became a human being. Many people don't accept that Jesus is God, especially considering the way he died. You are further challenged to believe in the miracle that bread and wine are transformed into Jesus, allowing him to feed you. At times doubt gnaws at your faith. You question what the Church teaches and are left in a quandary. You know that many other people, even good people, do not share your faith.

Whenever your faith wavers, don't worry. If you reach out your arms to me, I will shore up your faith so it doesn't collapse. Ask me to pray for you to the Holy Spirit, the one who made the Incarnation possible. This Holy Spirit who once filled the hearts of frightened apostles with faith, will fill your heart with it too.

ଔ *Talk to Mary about doubts you may have about the faith. She is a good listener.*

Why Mary?
Maternity of Our Lady

October 11

My child, people might wonder why God chose a woman to come into the world. He could have simply appeared out of thin air, fully grown. Instead God decided to come as a vulnerable, dependent baby and call a human being "Mother." In doing so, God most completely identified with us. He learned what it is to go through all stages of life. He also knows the love of a mother as well as love for a mother. There's a terrible, humbling beauty about this plan of God.

Because I was the woman God chose to be his mother, I was made sinless and was granted privileges. A special privilege flowing from my role of Mother of God is that I became the mother of all people. I am your mother. Proudly and happily I care for you with maternal love, protecting you and interceding for you. As I guided and supported Jesus for most of his life, allow me to hold your hand as you grow older. My love for you will be unfailing all the days of your life.

CR *Talk to Mary about how she has shown herself your mother.*

Adding Excitement

October 12

My child, welcome each new day as an adventure loaded with possibilities. From minute to minute you never know what engrossing project you will embark on, what interesting person will step into your life, what challenge you will meet up with, or what surprising event will occur. Still, circumstances are not the architect of your life as much as you are. Add excitement and beauty as spice to your life. Be daring and go on an escapade. Risk telling people you love them. Do something you've never done before.

To make your days even more splendid, fill them with bringing the good news of Jesus to people. Ask me to help you to devise creative strategies to share your faith. Introduce others to Jesus by mentioning him. Perform little acts of love and random acts of kindness to draw people to him. Be ingenious in involving others in the practice of your faith. When you take advantage of opportunities to witness to my son, your ordinary day becomes extraordinary. You go to bed tired but satisfied, knowing that you are a day closer to the everlasting day. And I will thank you.

ରେ *Talk to Mary about ways you can make the most out of every day.*

Children
Our Lady of Fatima

October 13

My child, like my son, I have a particular fondness for children. Their sweet innocence and simplicity are so attractive. They trust others wholeheartedly and are quick to show their love. They don't act superior or snobbish, and their spontaneity is delightful.

I recall when you were a child learning to talk and walk and discovering the world. As I watched you grow to become the beautiful person you are today, I prayed that you would retain the rare quality of childlikeness.

I was angry when you were mistreated as a youngster and when you were pressured to do wrong. Jesus said that if you led a child astray, it would be better if a great millstone were fastened around your neck and you were drowned.[56] I ask you to do something difficult. Forgive anyone who harmed you when you were a child. Pray for them. And cherish the children in your life. Do what you can to protect them and teach them about Jesus and his way. Respect each little person. Love boys and girls with the same solicitous love that I have for you.

ᙅ *Tell Mary the childlike characteristic you desire to develop.*

---

[56] Matthew 18:6

About Slights and Slurs

October 14

My child, occasionally you feel like an outsider. Your friends go to a party, but you weren't invited. Someone mocks the outfit you're wearing. A popular rival is chosen over you. You overhear an unkind remark about you. Your successes are not acknowledged. You long to be part of the circle of laughing people, but you stand alone.

Not being accepted or appreciated crushes your spirit, deflates your self-confidence, and makes you suffer. How I want to alleviate your pain! Know that I'm aware of your special qualities and your little and large triumphs that might be hidden from others. To me you are like a rare and lovely flower. You are a miracle made by God and belonging to him. What does it matter if everyone around you ignores you when God and I think the world of you? You are a beloved member of our family.

Climb out of that dark pit you were pushed into either deliberately or unintentionally. Stand tall and lift your head. I encircle you with my arms, darling. Sense my love soaking into you and washing away your hurts.

℞ *Confide in Mary your hurtful experiences of being slighted and ask her to help you to rise above them.*

Infinite Mercy

October 15

My child, when you fall into sin, you are angry with yourself and ashamed. You wish you had better control over your words and actions. You might be embarrassed and shy about approaching me. Never let sin come between us. I understand your frailty and how easy it is to be trapped in Satan's web. You do things you really do not want to do. But God's mercy is boundless.

No sin is too terrible for your heavenly Father to forgive. Listen to the consoling words of the prophet Micah. He said that God "delights in showing clemency" and "will tread our iniquities under foot" and "will cast all our sins into the depths of the seas."[57] You are not beyond the scope of God's compassion and love.

As for the future, dear, cheer up and bravely move on. I will be praying that you sidestep the stumbling blocks on your path. If it happens that you do trip, I will be there to steady you. If you fall flat on your face, I will help you up. Rely on me to conduct you with pleasure to your final destiny.

❧ *Talk to Mary about a sin you struggle to avoid.*

---

[57] Micah 7:18–19

Pure of Heart
Purity of Our Lady

October 16

My child, in describing those people who are worthy of God's kingdom, Jesus declared, "Blessed are the pure in heart, for they will see God."[58] He was referring to people who keep free from the taint of sin. His statement was correct. Through the goodness of God, I am the purest one ever created and now I am blessed — totally happy in the presence of God in his kingdom.

The holier you are, the closer you are to God. At your baptism, you were pure of heart, full of grace. You were aflame with God's life and love. As time passed, sin periodically stained your heart, creating a rift between you and your heavenly Father. I felt sorry for you.

Strive your utmost, sweetheart, to keep your heart aglow with God's love. I will help you keep the fire stoked. Then anyone who comes into contact with you will be warmed and may also catch fire. Best of all, at the end of time you will be numbered among the citizens of heaven. You will be with me forever.

ଔ *Tell Mary you wish to imitate her purity of heart and be full of grace.*

---

[58] Matthew 5:8

Divine Pattern

October 17

My child, the adversities you run up against are puzzling to you. Faithfully you are trying to live as Jesus taught, and so your difficulties are a mystery. Don't worry. The things that cause you grief and frustration are nothing less than part of God's pattern for your life. I noticed that when I wove cloth on my loom, the designs that gave me the most trouble were the ones that turned out to be the most striking. You might not realize it at the time, but as you engage a struggle and patiently accept it, you are in the process of creating a product that you and I will be proud of — a life of stunning beauty.

While in the midst of trials, you are only aware of the knots and messiness in the fabric of your life. That, dear, is the view from underneath. What I behold is the lovely design that is taking shape on the topside.

To bear up under adverse circumstances, stretch out your arms to me. I will obtain for you the grace to endure. Together we will craft your life into something beautiful for God.

ଓ *Ask Mary to accompany you through a difficult situation confronting you.*

The Blessing of Solitude

October 18

My child, when you are swallowed up for quite a while in a crowd of people laughing and talking, when you are drained by others making demands of you, or when you are caught in a maelstrom of activities, you probably crave some solitude. You need to catch your breath and get your bearings. So be good to yourself and withdraw from the world for a while. Don't feel guilty about doing this. Jesus was wise enough to hide sometimes from the throngs of people who followed him.

Going off by yourself affords you the respite you require for your health and sanity. Away from the din of people's voices and the pressure their presence exerts on you, you can recoup your energy. You are also freer to commune with God and with me.

Settle down in solitude and soak in the peace. Breathe deeply and relax. Be conscious of us from the world beyond—your heavenly Father and I—regarding you lovingly. With us as your only companions, you will be refreshed. You will have more vigor in coping with whatever life deals you.

ભ *Solicit Mary's help in taking opportunities to enjoy solitude once in a while.*

A Vessel of Love

October 19

My child, God made you in his image, and God is love. This God of love dwells in you. Moreover, you came into being through the love of your parents. You are to let love pour out from you onto the people around you. Every day I prayed the Shema, which calls us to love God with our whole being. Jesus identified this as the greatest commandment. But as the second greatest, he named loving your neighbor. I fulfill both of these laws by loving you, dearest.

It's a joy to love someone who loves you. But extending love to certain people is a colossal feat. Ask me for the power to love those who are unloved, people who are marginalized, the dirty, the crude, and the mean, the belligerent child, the woman whose dog damages your garden, and the teenager who broke into your house.

Don't let the streams of your love drive up. Be generous in acting as a conduit of love to all of God's children. Some might not return your love or appreciate it, but that shouldn't daunt you. Imagine if the world were flooded with love. That would be heaven on earth.

ଔ *Talk to Mary about people you find difficult to love.*

Fertile Soil

October 20

My child, be soft, fertile soil for God's Word to sink into and grow deep roots. I always loved hearing God speak to me through Moses and the prophets in our Hebrew Scriptures. After Jesus left home, I sometimes went to where he was teaching. I would listen attentively to his wise words and then return home and ponder them. I advise you to do the same, darling.

At Mass when Scripture is read, be all ears. Don't daydream or think "I know this story" and instead of listening, begin planning your next meal. You are different from the last time you heard it, and so different things will strike you. God's word is alive and powerful. Listen for the message God has for you and let it change your life. When you pray alone, read from the Bible and be open to what God says. Relish his words.

When you allow God's word to be implanted in your heart, it will blossom and bear fruit. People will be nourished by your virtues, your goodness. You will come to resemble me more and more and be a blessing to your world that so needs it.

ભ *Talk to Mary about the role of Scripture in your life.*

Possessions

October 21

My child, when accumulating possessions is an addiction, they possess you. If you are the victim of the compulsion to buy more and more things, ask me to help you rein it in. The poor would be delighted to receive the extra clothes and shoes cramming your closets, the unused kitchenware, and the profusion of objects decorating your rooms. Owning less makes you more lighthearted. You do not have as much to worry about or clean.

I don't want you to be dragged down by excess baggage en route to paradise. Hear me spurring you on to assess your belongings and thin them out if necessary.

Jesus taught, "Whoever has two coats must share with anyone who has none."[59] When he died, he owned one tunic that I had lovingly made for him. He said our treasure should be in heaven. My son meant accumulate good deeds. Focus on the one all-important possession, God. He is enough to satisfy the aching longing of your heart. When you have God, you have all you need.

Ask Mary to help you make wise decisions as your sort through your belongings.

---

[59] Luke 3:11

God's Work

October 22

My child, today when there is so much bad news, Jesus depends on you to broadcast the good news. That is the mission you inherited the day you were baptized a Christian. Spread the word that God loves everyone and sent Jesus to restore our hope for eternal happiness. You needn't do this in dramatic ways. You don't have to work miracles. Simply lead other people to Jesus by the light of your life. Let your faith and love radiate from your face. Practice kindness, forgiveness, and peacemaking.

If you are intimidated by this responsibility, take courage in the knowledge that God will work through you. You will accomplish things you can't do alone and might not even understand. Let me play an active role, too, as you carry out your mission. If you wish, I can go before the throne of my son and present your requests for stronger faith and courage. His Spirit can inspire you to know how best to enlighten people.

The more you invest in this great work of Jesus, the happier you will be and the happier you will make other people, including me.

ભ *Ask Mary to pray that you have the grace to be a zealous missionary disciple.*

Giving Thanks

October 23

My child, as you go through your day, offer thanks for what our good God gives you or allows to happen. As soon as you awake, thank God for another sunrise. Thank him for the clothes you put on, the water you use, and the birds you hear singing. At each meal you enjoy that day, give God thanks for providing it. As you encounter people—family members, neighbors, coworkers—thank God for adding them to your life,

Be alert during the day to small favors God bestows on you. He dispenses them lavishly, but you need good eyesight to spot them. Each time you experience a blessing—catch yourself from falling, locate a missing book, or receive unexpected help from a friend—thank God. Even thank him for sufferings, for they have benefits. If you cultivate this practice of expressing gratitude, your day will be woven through with prayer. You will be more conscious of God's love for you.

Remember to thank God too for my presence in your life, one of his most precious gifts to you. All day long I am near you, protecting you, aiding you, and encircling you with my love.

ᐒ *Express thanks to Mary for her tender, loving care.*

Blossoming

October 24

My child, you might consider your life plain and routine, devoid of any fantastic achievements. You may think of yourself as a bland, uninteresting person. Banish such thoughts, sweetheart. There is no need for you to feel lowly and insignificant. God is at work in you every minute of your existence. His divine life is increasing daily in your soul. You are becoming more and more the beautiful person God expects you to be. That in itself is a grand thing.

I am God's accomplice as he continues to create you. With a mother's love, I dote on you. I coax you to develop the positive traits latent in your heart. I beg God for the graces you need. As devotedly as I raised Jesus to maturity, I help you perfect yourself until you reach your full potential. Like the little mustard seed that grows into a sizable bush, you are gradually gaining strength and power. In time you will blossom and be ready to join me in the kingdom of our Father.

ɔ *Ponder how God has worked in you recently. Talk to Mary about a virtue you think you particularly need at this point in your life.*

Living Faith

October 25

My child, saying "I believe" has implications. Not only does it entail trusting God with all your heart but also living as Jesus taught. It is an illusion to think that by merely saying words you can expect to be saved. Faith is useless unless it is awake and active. I long to stir up your faith, dear. The more often you practice it, the stronger it will be when it is tried by pain and sorrow, your own transgressions, or by unbelievers attempting to poke holes in it.

You practice faith by celebrating the Eucharist with me, by continually building your relationship with God, by responding to your poor and suffering brothers and sisters, and by resisting temptations.

I assure you, your faith is not a fantasy. There is another world awaiting you. My son's death transformed your death into a birth. Keep living your faith so it doesn't wither and die. When you are too busy, tired, or lazy to do so, call on me for help. I know what is at stake—your eternal life—and I want you to clinch it, dear.

ൡ *Take an honest look at the quality of your faith. Talk to Mary about it.*

Healing for Your Heart

October 26

My child, are you hurting? Maybe someone has rejected your love and wounded your heart. Perhaps a barrage of sorrows has fallen on you, leaving you on the verge of screaming. Maybe you are disappointed with yourself for not living up to your ideals. If you find yourself in any of these situations, or another one is causing you pain and distress, you could use my maternal comfort. Don't hesitate to turn to me.

I will escort you out from the parched, burning desert you currently inhabit into the cool, lush garden of peace. I will cup your beloved face in my hands, look directly into your eyes, and reassure you that all will be well. Relax in my healing presence. Be immersed in the flow of my love and feel the tension leave your body.

Take the long view of your life's journey. Your road zigzags and at times is perilous. You had smooth stretches before and you will again. Grasping tightly onto my compassionate hand, go forward with a firm step. You are walking into a future that never ends, a future that holds much joy.

℘ *Are you passing through a painful time in your life? Tell Mary how much you are hurting.*

Speaking to Mary

October 27

My child, I look forward to the time we spend together. Sometimes you are caught up in the myriad demands of your busy life and still squeeze in time to speak with me. I appreciate that. As for me, I have all the time in the world, and I'm easily accessible—right there beside you.

In our conversations, please feel free to share with me whatever is on your mind. Be totally uninhibited. I will not be shocked or laugh at you. I'm interested in your deepest feelings and thoughts, those you usually don't reveal to others. You can be comfortable and relaxed with me. Others may judge you, but I never will. My aim as your mother is to be your encourager, your consoler, and your counselor.

I am thrilled when you include me in your life. We enjoy being in the presence with those we love, and I have enormous love for you, darling. When you talk to me, time speeds by and is always too short. I hope you feel the same way.

 Spend time right now with Mary. Share with her the secrets of your heart.

Life Unraveling

October 28

My child, you were coasting along fine. Life was good. Your carefully laid plans were unfolding right on schedule. Then, without warning, one by one various aspects of your life came undone. Maybe the man who was going to purchase your house changed his mind, or you failed your driving test. Perhaps your flight to Rome was cancelled. It could be your spouse walked out on you. Whatever happened to spoil your life left you teetering on the edge of the unknown. I know the feeling. My marriage plans were turned upside-down after the Angel Gabriel visited me.

Whenever your plans are ruined, you can depend on your heavenly Father to step in and replace them with a superior plan. Keep your chin up and wait for his masterplan to unfold. In the meantime, feel my arm around you, steadying you to face what is around the corner. It helps if you are flexible and can easily adapt to new circumstances. I will pray that you have the grace to see things God's way and trust him as implicitly as I did.

ℜ *Has one or more of your plans been foiled? Talk to Mary about it.*

Miracles

October 29

My child, you may wish you lived when I did so you could witness miracles Jesus performed or even benefit from one yourself. You might ask, Where are miracles today?

Open your eyes and ears, my dear. Miracles occur to verify the holiness of saints. Ordinary people relate accounts of impossible things happening. For example, a tumor inexplicably disappears. At my Lourdes shrine spiritual miracles take place regularly. Hardened hearts are turned to God, and grace to bear afflictions flows as freely as the waters. Don't be shy about asking God for a miracle. Be sure to ask for my support in requesting it.

You are surrounded by ordinary miracles. See the hand of God at work in natural wonders. It's a miracle every time a baby enters the world. When coincidences occur against all odds, they are little miracles. Then there is the astounding miracle that you are privy to every day if you wish: Jesus comes in the form of bread and wine.

Of course, you shouldn't ask for miracles in order to believe in God. Faith is believing without seeing. I'd say that having faith is a kind of miracle.

ᄋᔓ *Talk to Mary about a miracle you would like to see happen.*

When People Let You Down

October 30

My child, by now you have learned that you can't always depend on people to keep their promises. They say they will help you, but then don't follow through. They agree to come to your party or meeting, but then don't show up. You look to people to speak up for you, and they are as silent as a stone. That is discouraging. Imagine what our good God feels like when his children break their promises to him!

Don't allow a few bad experiences sour you on the whole human race. There are plenty of people who are faithful to their commitments and to you. Recall instances when you were grateful, and maybe surprised, because others kept their word and supported you.

Dear, I am one person who will always be faithful to you. When you turn to me for help, I will be there. I will hand over your requests for special graces to my son. I will not let you down. And when other people disappoint you, I will soothe your wounded heart. I will also prompt you to forgive them. That is what Christians do.

ભ *Share with Mary times you were hurt by others' betrayal or lack of support. Ask her to obtain the grace to forgive them.*

Fright

October 31

My child, you are no stranger to fear. At times you are scared to death. You or a loved one might be facing major surgery. A fierce thunderstorm with flashes of lightning and the threat of tornadoes might be bearing down on your house. Maybe you are about to take a test or be interviewed. Your heart pounds, and you break out in a sweat. Other times you are frightened by people who dislike you and act like monsters intent on doing you harm. Then too memories of your own wicked deeds can haunt you and make you fear for your salvation.

Whenever you are scared, I am alarmed. I long to comfort you and fill your terrified heart with peace. Run to me, darling, and burrow your head in my shoulder. I will wrap you in my protective mantle. Safe in the shelter of my loving arms, you will stop trembling and calm down. With my help, you will conquer your fear and be ready to walk into your future — whatever it holds — with confidence, peace, and even joy. Trust me.

ભ *Does some threat loom in your life, disturbing your peace? Talk to Mary about it.*

November

Mary, Queen of Saints
Feast of All Saints

November 1

My child, in a homily on this day in 2014, Pope Francis said, "In the great assembly of saints, God has wanted to reserve the first place for the Mother of Jesus." He called me "the center of the communion of saints, as the singular guardian of the bond of the universal Church with Christ." You probably don't usually think of me as St. Mary, but as a citizen of heaven, that is what I am. No one carried out God's will more perfectly than I. Despite the many challenges I encountered in my vocation as God's mother, I never gave up.

My wish now is that someday you will join the rest of us saints in heaven. There we will be united forever in love and doing what we were created for: praising and glorifying our Creator.

Pray to me, your loving mother, and to your brothers and sisters in Christ, for the graces you need each day. In your vocation, you will meet obstacles. Don't let them keep you from striving to live a saintly life. My son and I look forward to seeing you here with us eventually.

ଔ *Talk to Mary about a saint you admire and wish to imitate.*

When Loved Ones Die

November 2

My child, when someone you love dies, it can be devastating. Although your tears stop flowing, your heart still aches, sometimes for years. You miss that person whose departure leaves a gaping hole in your life. I understand. I had to say goodbye to my beloved Joseph too early. And then I endured the severe pain of losing my only child. It's sad when parents outlive their children.

As you grieve, people speak words of comfort to you, but they don't penetrate your frozen heart. Your faith offers consolation, assuring you that you will be reunited with your loved one someday. But even that doesn't help much during the hours when sorrow first overwhelms you. You long to be with that person right now.

Words beyond what your faith and Jesus tell you fail me. I simply enfold you in my loving arms and weep with and for you. Later, when people stop expressing sympathy by offering Masses and bringing over casseroles, I still remember your sorrow. But like you, I also remember the gift that departed loved one was for you. Cherish the memories of your time with him or her.

ख *Do you miss someone who passed into the next world? Talk to Mary about it.*

Being Countercultural

November 3

My child, it isn't too comfortable being a follower of Jesus. In fact, it is becoming increasingly difficult in the midst of your cultural revolution. Jesus did foretell that you could expect the cross and persecution. When you uphold his teachings, your positions on certain issues run counter to the opinions of modern society. Some people think your views strange. You sometimes are ostracized or mocked. That is the price you pay for being a Christian.

At times you must protest immoral acts and not fear the consequences. When you have the courage to do so, I pat you on the back and say, "Congratulations." Another tactic for changing people's opinions is to promote the beauty your faith holds and its vision of a better world. That ought to attract people.

I will be your support as you take a firm stand in the face of opposing ideas and refuse to compromise. Resist the cultural currents and set about renewing the world. I will inspire you to speak up and explain the plan Jesus has to offer. Let me partner with you to restore creation to its original goodness and lead people to salvation.

ଔ *Talk to Mary about your experiences of being criticized for your position on controversial issues.*

Kindness

November 4

My child, you never know how much a little act of kindness means to someone. It has power to bring out the sun on a sad, dreary day. It lifts spirits mired in a morass of bad misfortunes. When Joseph and I were homeless in Bethlehem, one overwrought innkeeper who was dealing with a full house was still kind enough to offer us his stable. What a difference that made in my life!

Never let an opportunity for showing kindness to someone pass you by. I will call your attention to it. With God's grace, you will summon the time and effort to perform the deed. When your act of kindness backfires, when someone spurns it or resents it, no matter. You have the satisfaction of knowing you did the right and loving thing. You still add to your treasure in heaven.

Aim to build a reputation for being kind. Go out of your way to do a favor, overlook faults, forgive easily, say encouraging words, and give gifts. People will then be comfortable in your presence. I will be happy because kindness is a fruit of the Holy Spirit and shows you are on the right track to paradise.

෫ *Reminisce with Mary the times people have shown you kindness.*

Spending Time

November 5

My child, a specific number of years are allotted to you. You are free to spend them as you wish. I urge you not to squander them, but to make the most of them. The glitter of the world can blind you to the really important things in life. It tempts you to devote an unreasonable number of hours to being entertained and to enjoying its pleasures. But with me at your side, you have power to resist and make wise choices.

How I would like to help you to enrich your days by developing your talents; by strengthening your relationships with your family members; by serving others, especially the needy; and by spending time with Jesus and me. Then at the end of your life when you look back over it, you will be glad that you invested most of your time in these worthwhile occupations instead of frittering it away in nonessentials. You would have lived a full life pleasing to God, who gave you the gift of life. Let me be your gentle guide in determining your priorities. Then ask me to assist you in living by them.

℞ *Talk to Mary about any adjustments needed in how you spend your time.*

When Dreams Are Dashed

November 6

My child, your dreams do not always come true. You are exhilarated at the prospect of seeing a popular play, but on the way to the theater, you are in an accident. Someone tells you there's a good chance you will win first prize in a contest, but then you don't even win honorable mention. You anticipate becoming a famous singer, but a friend informs you that your voice is flat. When such things occur in your life, I commiserate with you. I wish all your hopes were fulfilled.

The important thing, dear, is how you react. Accept your disappointment gracefully and if possible hide it from others. Trust me to see you through your pain, and trust God to be working behind the scenes mysteriously to fulfill his monumental dream for you, namely, eternal happiness.

The next time what you hope for doesn't materialize, don't waste a lot of time bemoaning the fact. Don't let it ruin your optimism. Create a new dream for yourself. You have power to direct the course of your life towards ultimate success, especially with me behind you.

ॐ *Tell Mary about a disappointment you had and how you dealt with it.*

Cooperating with Grace

November 7

My child, you are showered with an abundance of grace. The Holy Spirit often nudges you to do good. Be open to these graces and act promptly. Many a time I was inspired to leave the hustle and bustle of my daily chores go in order to attend to a neighbor in need. For example, while milking our goat, the idea would come to me to take some milk to the elderly widow Sarah down the road who had no goat. I had to ignore the devil when he presented reasons why I shouldn't do that spontaneous act of love.

When similar notions flit across your mind, don't suppress them. Imitate me, your mother, in being open to the Spirit and cooperating with him. Each good act you do will be like a stone tossed into a pond. Ripples will emanate from it that influence more people than you know. It will make a difference in the universe.

When you receive an actual grace, hear me say to you, "Move." Don't waste time weighing the pros and cons, or the opportunity might pass.

ℭ *Talk over with Mary times you responded to graces and times you ignored them.*

Let Mary Support You
Patronage of Our Lady
November 8

My child, the earliest prayer to me that has come down to you begins "We fly to thy patronage." This short but powerful prayer was found on a third-century Coptic papyrus describing a Christmas liturgy.

When you pray this prayer, you are trusting in my patronage. A patron of the arts supports a person, usually financially. You are working on a masterpiece: your life. I am your unfailing patron who provides things more valuable than money for you. When you need something, rely on me to obtain it for you. When you are in danger, I will defend you. When you give me entrance into the dark places of your life, I will comfort you and give you the strength you keep to keep your balance.

It would give me pleasure to hear you praying the early prayer frequently. I'm not only your patron but your mother who loves you. Allowing me to be a true mother to you opens a wellspring of joy in the depths of your being.

ᴄ℞ *Tell Mary how you would like her to show herself your patron. Pray: We fly to thy patronage, O holy Mother of God; despise not our petitions in our necessities, but deliver us always from all dangers, O glorious and blessed Virgin."*

What Others Think of You

November 9

My child, your self-image is formed to some degree by what others think of you. Do not be held hostage by their impressions, which can be distorted or completely false. For example, they might incorrectly assume you are dull, unintelligent, lazy, or egotistical. Do not live down to low assessments like these.

You know who you are, your thoughts, motivations, and gifts better than anyone on earth. You have the lights to make decisions for yourself that no one else has. If you recognize that there is a grain of truth in an adverse comment about you, take it to heart as a signpost on your way to an improved life. On the other hand, if you realize that people attribute shining qualities to you that you do not possess, aim to acquire them.

What matters most is what God thinks of you. I can tell you that you are the apple of his eye. Sure, you have your faults and you live in a fragile and broken world, but God acknowledges your struggles to be better. To me you are a beloved child in the making and I am here to ensure that you become the best possible.

ന *Talk to Mary about what you perceive to be your best and worst traits.*

Concept of God

November 10

My child, you will never comprehend fully who God is. Think of the universe so vast that no one knows where it ends. God, who created those countless galaxies is far greater than this. Consider the intricate complexity of creatures on earth. We stand in awe at God's wisdom and ingenuity that designed the exquisite daisy and the odd-looking camel. Whenever rolling thunder shook the earth or I gazed at the massive Mount Hermon in the distance, I was reminded of the immense power of God. He is the ultimate good, truth, and beauty.

Even though God is almighty, you never need to fear him. At heart, he is pure, burning love. You, dear, are the object of God's infinite love. He knows your name and invites you to call him Father. God is full of loving compassion. If you offend him, God is quick to forgive. He swoops you up joyfully and holds you next to his cheek.

God made me the vessel of his love for you. Not only did God restore eternal life through me, but he uses me to lead you to him. My prayers for you are unceasing.

ભ *Speak to Mary about strengthening your ties to her and to God. Pray: Mary, make me live in God, with God, and for God.*

Missionary Discipleship

November 11

My child, God has chosen you to bring amazing news to the world. By virtue of your baptism, you have the privilege of delivering the message that God loves us, redeemed us, and awaits us in his kingdom. You are also designated to be the agent of peace, justice, and love to the people in your era. In other words, you are called to participate in God's work of salvation.

Your task might seem overwhelming, as daunting as my strange and wonderful role of being Mother of God. The grace of God empowered me, a young unlettered woman, to fulfill my role, and you can count on grace to enable you too.

When you become discouraged at your lack of success in handing on the faith, or when you tire from swimming against the tide, ask me to appeal to God to let abundant grace flow into you. When your own faith falters, my prayers can bolster it, making it robust again. I can help reorient you to God and to the purpose for which you were put on earth. You are endowed with natural gifts and the supernatural gifts of the Holy Spirit. Use all of those gifts well, dear.

ᖇ *Talk to Mary about your efforts to spread the Gospel and promote God's reign on earth.*

God's Will

November 12

My child, be attuned to God's will, which is far superior than yours. Be smart and adjust your will to align with his all-wise one. The rhythm of your life might occasionally be disrupted by a change of plans or an emergency. What happens to you might make no sense at first glance. You might balk and resist it. On the day God broke into my peaceful life in Nazareth and made me his mother, I was dumbfounded and puzzled. Still, I immediately replied, "Let it be." May this be the refrain in your life, darling: "Let it be."

Before any undertaking and before making a decision, ask the Holy Spirt for guidance. Only when you surrender yourself to his sweet power will you achieve the profound serenity you desire. The results will astonish you, if not here, then hereafter. Because in the Garden of Gethsemane my dear son submitted to the will of the Father, all creation was redeemed and restored. What he dreaded became the source of eternal life for all.

I pray that you imitate Jesus and me in complying with God's will and loving it. Whenever it seems too much for you, know that I will be walking arm in arm with you along the way.

ॐ *Talk to Mary about an aspect of God's will you are struggling to accept.*

Soaring Like an Eagle

November 13

My child, the prophet Isaiah said that those who wait for the Lord will renew their strength and soar like an eagle.[60] When you place your hope in God, you have remarkable strength and power that people who rely only on themselves or other human beings lack. God, for whom a thousand years are as a single day, sometimes has you wait for something for what seems like eons. Look how long the Israelites waited for the Messiah.

If you maintain your trust in God, who is always faithful, eventually you will not be disappointed. In the meantime, buoyed up by hope, you will rise above any troubles that come your way. You will not creep along day after day or collapse under the weight of your trials, weakened by despair. Instead you will soar like an eagle flying over storms. You will ride on the wind currents unleashed by the Holy Spirit.

I waited nine months for Jesus to make an appearance. I wait now with you for his coming at the end of time. Expecting his arrival gives meaning to your life and motivates you to pursue holiness with joy and zeal.

ᘒ *Ask Mary to pray that you keep your hopes securely pinned on God and his promises.*

---

[60] Isaiah 40:31

Bound for Glory

November 14

My child, when you walk along day after day, experiencing highs and lows, remember that you are bound for glory. You are on your way to an indescribable life beyond your wildest hopes and dreams. When you cross the finish line, the trials and problems of this life will disappear. You will be enveloped in a powerful, never-ending love that fills you with untold joy and peace.

The degree of your future happiness depends on how you handle the events that transpire while you are on earth. Naturally, darling, I wish you the greatest joy. That is why I travel with you through this life, guiding you in matters great and small. Whenever you are bogged down with burdens, shift them onto my shoulders. I will pray fervently that you have the courage to go forward with determination. Whenever you are tempted to veer from the right path, count on me to steer you toward that goal that at heart you desire, but sometimes forget.

When you arrive at heaven's gates, I will welcome you and clothe you in the white robes of a saint. Yes, this is possible, dear, for you have a powerful advocate before God's throne, his mother.

ℭ℞ *Talk to Mary about the challenges you meet as you keep your eyes on the goal of heaven.*

Listening

November 15

My child, for most of your day you are surrounded by noise. Traffic, music, television, phones, people talking and laughing—all put a damper on the voice of your heavenly Father. They drown out the voices of the needy who cry out for relief from their suffering.

Come away with me for a slice of your day, and let us sit in silence. Apart from the hustle and bustle, listen to what God wants to say in the chamber of your heart. He may have a special mission for you. He may suggest a way to become more like the person you would like to be. Undoubtedly, your heavenly Father will assure you of his undying love.

By listening carefully to God in silence, my dear, you will be more likely to detect his soft voice in the cacophony of everyday life too. I heard him not only in the angel but in Joseph, Elizabeth, and Simeon. God speaks to you through the friend who gives you advice, the book you happen to read, and the unexpected phone call with a request for help. Be attuned to him. I, who am called the listening virgin, will assist you in paying attention to God and responding.

☙ *When have you heard the Lord speak to you? Talk to Mary about it.*

Growing Weary

November 16

My child, sometimes you are bone tired. The demands of daily life wore you down, and you are disillusioned with life. You wonder if this is all there is: an endless round of routine duties with no prospect of relief in sight. Maybe enduring chronic pain adds to your discouragement.

When you hit rock bottom in contemplating your life, that is when I most want to be mother to you. Rest your head on my shoulder. I will caress you, comfort you, and encourage you to go on, one baby step at a time.

It's all right to feel depressed at times. Remember that you are not alone. I pray before the throne of God that hope will bloom again in your heart. Trust me. One day the clouds will part and the sun will once more warm you with its rays. You will be at peace and even smile again—a real smile, not a forced one. In the meantime, be faithful to God and to your commitments. That is important even when you are tired. The more successful you are at ploughing through the rough patches of life, the more abundant your blessings will be. And who knows? A marvelous thing might be waiting for you tomorrow.

ଓ *Talk to Mary about how you might get through difficult times gracefully.*

Thought Control

November 17

My child, all day long your mind is churning. Most thoughts arise unbidden, stimulated by what your senses perceive or popping up from your subconscious. Your memory is an ever-deepening wellspring of thoughts that seep into your mind. Good thoughts lead to good acts and happiness, while bad thoughts are the road to bad acts and ultimately sadness. Naturally, dear, I would like you to be a font of positive thoughts and full of joy.

Control your mind to focus on the good in people. Ignore their bad features and resist what is even worse: searching for their faults. Concentrate on the good aspects of experiences instead of the bad. Block input that would poison your mind with dangerous thoughts, such as immoral movies, shows, and literature.

I will pray to the Holy Spirit to see that many of your thoughts originate with him. This guest of your soul has powerful influence over your mind and consequently your behavior. My wish is that you would often think of me and my son. Ponder our lives and decide how you could imitate us. And think about how we are alive and with you now, guiding your life and loving you.

ଔ *Ask Mary to help you monitor your thoughts and entertain only the beneficial ones.*

Being Versus Doing

November 18

My child, your relatives and friends may hold high positions and be achieving great things. Compared to them, you might feel somewhat inadequate and suffer a twinge of jealousy. But unless you are shirking work, don't bother rushing about striving to do more. You might give yourself a heart attack or an ulcer. If circumstances beyond your control limit your activity, such as age or illness, don't regret it. Your heavenly Father and I are more interested in who you are than what you do.

When you do all you are reasonably capable of, be content and at peace. We don't expect you to do more. You are important and valuable simply because of who you are and whose you are. Hone the splendid qualities you possess. Inspire people by your cheerfulness, your patience, your attitude of thanksgiving, and your love. That will be enough for you to be a success in our eyes. To attain a heavenly reward, earthly awards and famous feats are not required. A soul sparkling with virtues is.

As you work at being, I will be at your side, helping you to become a beautiful person and cheering you on.

℘ *Talk to Mary about your goals in life.*

Confidence
Mother of Divine Providence

November 19
Saturday before the Third Sunday of November

My child, God, oversees the smooth running of the universe. Jesus said that no sparrow falls to the ground without the Father's knowledge.[61] God is working through everything that happens to you. Trust in his goodness and wisdom guiding every facet of your life, your joys and your sorrows, the people you encounter and the situations that enmesh you. The pain you suffer and the mistakes you make do not impede the progress of his plan. Mysteriously he draws good from them to further his purpose: to bring you into closer union with him.

Believe in divine providence as I did when I didn't understand the strange and sometimes frightening course my life took. View every occurrence as holding potential for grace, a gift from your heavenly Father. He loves you very much and directs everything in your favor. You have only to cooperate. Don't be surprised if God intervenes in your life with a miracle, especially after I intercede for you. Place your confidence in us and our loving care.

cs *Talk to Mary about times you felt God's hand at work.*

---

[61] Matthew 10:29

Be Jesus

November 20

My child, Jesus depends on you, his disciple, to make him present in your world. Be a person of love. Show compassion to the homeless, the helpless, and the hungry. Work for justice in your city, the nation, and the world. Promote peace in your family and among friends and acquaintances. Live with integrity, rejecting the opinions of the world when necessary. Spread the message of Jesus' death and resurrection so others come to know him and have hope.

To be Jesus is to be God-like. I admit that is a challenging mission. You might wish to protest, "I'm not ready," "I'm not good enough," or "I don't have the gifts for that." Those would be lame excuses I hope I never hear from you, darling. Be a dynamic Christian, not one who is content with mediocrity, and you will be a blessing to others. Let this be your greatest ambition.

When you stagger under the weight of your responsibility, lean on me for support. My love for you will fuel your resolve to do your part in bringing about God's kingdom of peace and justice on earth.

ൟ *Who can you be Jesus to today? Talk with Mary about the possibilities.*

All for God
Presentation *of Mary*

November 21

My child, to emphasize my total consecration to God, a legend arose, recorded in the apocryphal *Protoevangelium of St. James.* It recounts that when I was three years old, my parents took me to the Jerusalem temple to present me to God. A sweet detail is that filled with grace, I danced with joy on the third step. The tradition is that I lived in the temple until I was twelve.

You were probably taken to church and baptized, consecrated to God. You become God's adopted child and a beloved member of his household. You were filled with grace, God's divine life. Most likely you were too little to understand the immensity of what occurred or to dance. I was happy on this great occasion and danced for you on heaven's stairway.

Now you realize the immense privilege it is to be a Christian. This thought should fill you with joy and gratitude. You belong to God in a special way, marked as his own for all eternity. I will prompt you to act in accord with the honor God bestowed on you. May your whole life, your every action praise him and give him glory.

ભ *Talk to Mary about why you are glad to be a Christian.*

Delight

November 22

My child, God has enhanced your world with countless fascinating things. As a child you were delighted by such ordinary things as an ant, a dandelion, and a puddle. Keep that childlike simplicity and be open to the marvels around you. Seek them out by hiking through the woods, by sitting quietly in your backyard and observing nature, or by visiting a zoo. Let God's unique gifts touch your heart until you tingle with joy.

Take delight in your body that could only be designed by a genius. Relish the various flavors of food you can taste. Watch how your skin miraculously heals itself after a cut. Appreciate the sense of well-being that follows a run or a brisk walk. Realize that God thought to paint the world with a full palette of colors instead of leaving it black and white, and that he gave you the eyes to see it.

As you walk about the earth today, I will be your companion and point out certain treasures. Then together we can praise and thank God for them.

ल *Talk to Mary about some created thing that gives you joy. Then tell her what you are able to do that delights you.*

Thanksgiving

November 23

My child, no matter how frequently you thank God or how effusive your expressions of gratitude are, they will never be enough. How do you thank someone who gave you life? How do you thank someone who forgives all your offenses? How do you thank someone who died for you? Here is an idea, dear. Live in such a way that God is glad that he made you, forgives you, and died for you. Surrender your whole life to him and do what pleases him. Even that would not be sufficient to thank almighty God for his goodness to you, but it is something.

God is so good that he has even provided a way to thank him: the Eucharist. This perfect prayer is the best way to thank God. At Mass, you are joined with the sacrifice of Jesus, which has infinite value and speaks volumes. I am there too, offering my thanks to God.

More than anyone else, I know the lengths God went to in order to save us. I know the depths of his love. I was an eyewitness. My prayer for you is that you have a heart full of gratitude and a prayer of thanks always on your lips.

ᘓ *Talk to Mary about ways you can show God you are thankful for his love and his gifts.*

Restlessness

November 24

My child, at times you feel restless and uncomfortable. You seek refuge in the lovely pleasures the world offers to quell these feelings. Nothing satisfies you. This restlessness is normal and shouldn't disturb you. It comes upon you because you are made for more, for greater things. You ache for God, the only one who can wholly extinguish your deep longing and fill you with peace. In him you will finally find rest.

In my loving care, you will grow closer to God. You will make him the center of your life. Little by little the God-shaped hole in your heart will be filled.

There is another kind of restlessness that I hope and pray takes hold of you, one spawned by the Spirit. The apostles burst on the scene in Jerusalem and went out to spread the good news of salvation. Likewise, knowing that God is the answer to our quest for happiness, you are compelled to share this knowledge. You will not be content until you do so. This is a holy restlessness.

Today may you be driven to draw someone to God by word or deed. I will help you, for I will not be at peace until all of my children are home safe.

ଓ *Talk to Mary about how you can bring people a step closer to God.*

Anxiety

November 25

My child, sometimes you work yourself into a frenzy anticipating an unfortunate or painful event that will or could possibly happen. Racked with anxiety, you feel sick, can't sleep or eat, and bite your fingernails. Then sometimes what you expected doesn't materialize. Your anxiety was all in vain. It is foolish to worry about the future. You do not even know if you will live to see the next day!

God gives you the grace and strength to cope with the hardships of the present day. When tomorrow arrives, he will see you through that day too. And I will accompany you moment by moment, ready to prop you up if troubles assail you.

Stay calm by focusing on what is happening now. Don't drain the power you have to meet today's calamities by wasting it on trials that may be only a figment of your imagination. The best remedy for anxiety is staunch faith in God's love for you and in my protective care.

cx *Do you tend to worry about the future? Talk to Mary about it and ask her to obtain for you the grace to grow in faith.*

Honesty

November 26

My child, if you took all the credit for your good features, your talents, your successes, or even your good works, that would be a bit ridiculous. Everything you are, have, and do stems from God. It is all his blessing, for which you owe him abundant thanks. My special privileges and my virtues were not my own doing either, but favors from God. Follow my footsteps by attributing your good points to their true source. Rather than being vain, be humbly grateful.

Don't bother boasting or flaunting your assets because tomorrow they could disappear. Also avoid acting greater than you really are. Burst the bubble of your pretentiousness, and you will be happier and more likable. Own up to your mistakes and laugh at yourself.

I pray that when you look in the mirror, you have the same vision of yourself that I do. I behold you as a unique, extraordinary individual with a few quirks. But I also see you as the wonderful handiwork of an inventive God who loves you beyond telling.

ᑫ *Talk over with Mary what you consider your good points and your flaws.*

Untapped Graces
Miraculous Medal of Mary Immaculate
November 27

My child, when I appeared to St. Catherine Labouré, I wore rings set with jewels. Rays emanated from some jewels unto the globe I stood on. I explained that the rays were graces, and the jewels that cast no rays stood for the graces for which no one had prayed. Dear, do tap into the power your heavenly Father gave me to help you. Have recourse to me when you are in dire straits or when you need just a little help. I will respond quickly, and God's grace will flow to you so wonderfully that it will take your breath away.

As you travel the roads of this life, I want you to walk with a spirit of gladness. My dream is that you live a full, vibrant life unperturbed by unsettling occurrences and problems. I am always here for you. I can't emphasize this enough. I showed mercy for the fragile, broken world, and I have utter compassion for you, darling. Your pleas for help go directly to my heart. Don't think twice about appealing to me, your loving mother.

cx *Share with Mary an intention close to you heart. Pray the prayer on the Miraculous Medal: O Mary, conceived without sin, pray for us who have recourse to you.*

Accepting Outsiders

November 28

My child, God has created human beings with a wonderful variety. They are of different sizes, shapes, colors, races, and nationalities. They have different backgrounds, cultures, social status, and opinions. You tend to be most comfortable with people who are like you. God's love is all embracing, and so should yours be. I encourage you to reach out to people who are different from you and mingle with them. Jesus did just that, even though it was frowned upon. He associated with sinners, lepers, and Samaritans.

Perhaps some of your neighbors are markedly different from you. Invite them to a meal or a party. Visit prisoners and the homeless who are in shelters. Are there people at work or in your family who are considered strange or eccentric? Befriend them. All people are my children whom I love. I will see that you have the courage to leave your comfort zone and spread the love of Christ to everyone, especially the unloved and unwanted. Backed by my prayers, you will make them feel accepted. You will further the kingdom of God where all are one.

ଔ *Speak to Mary about people in your sphere of influence who are marginalized and how you can include them.*

Faith in You

November 29

My child, you believe in God, but he also believes in you. He believes that you have within you the ability and the gumption to live a life of love and integrity. He believes you will participate wholeheartedly in his great work of salvation. He also believes that with my help and the help of the Holy Spirit, it is possible for you to attain eternal life.

You might not feel you are worthy of God's faith in you. Maybe you think you do not deserve his love and esteem and aren't able to meet up to his high expectations of you. Oftentimes your faults are all too glaring in your own eyes, or the task he sets before you looms like an unconquerable mountain.

When you are dejected and lack confidence, rush to my side. I will whisper in your ear, "You can do it. Together with me nothing is impossible for you." So cheer up. Don't mope over your faded dreams or concentrate on what you lack. Release your worries into my hands. God never gives up on you and neither do I.

ℭ *Talk to Mary about your progress in living as a true, committed follower of her son.*

Feeling Sorry for Yourself

November 30

My child, avoid being trapped in the snare of self-pity. You may be inclined to brood over injustices and misfortunes, to nurse grudges against those who slighted you, and to feel that you are taken for granted. You may compare yourself to others and concentrate on what you lack. Indulging in these practices, you begin to feel sorry for yourself. Continuing in this vein takes you in a downward spiral. You sink into melancholy and may turn into a grouch!

Wean yourself away from such self-destructive tendencies. Appreciate your good qualities. Send your bad memories into oblivion and look forward to making happy ones. Focus on the people who love you and have shown you kindness. Take shelter in my heart. I cherish you as a one-of-a-kind creation and my dear child.

I remind you that Jesus thought you were worth dying for. In fact, if you were the only one in the world, he still would have given his life to save you. Take comfort in the fact that he has prepared an incredible future for you.

ଔ *Talk to Mary about your desire to keep a positive attitude as your life unfolds.*

December

Mary, Morning Star

December 1

My child, I like my title Morning Star because it is lovely and because of what it signifies. The morning star in the sky is either the planet Venus or the star Sirius. Both of these heavenly bodies appear at the end of the dark night on the brink of dawn. Likewise, I was born at the end of Old Testament times when the world, separated from God by sin, was wrapped in darkness. Sirius is the brightest star, just as I, through God's grace, am the most radiant and highest of creatures. Like the morning star that heralds the brilliant, life-giving sun, I was the immediate precursor of the Son of God.

Now my rays of light and love fall on and around you, dear. Stars like the North Star serve as guides. During the day, look to me for assistance and counsel. Reflect my virtues — my faith, humility, and love — and you will not stray from the right road. A shining star led the Magi to Jesus in Bethlehem. Following me, the Morning Star, you will arrive at Jesus where he is now, in heaven, your future home.

ભ *Talk to Mary about an aspect of her beauty you wish to radiate.*

Discipleship Costs

December 2

My child, following Jesus exacts a toll that not everyone is willing to pay. He asks for your time, your talent, and your treasures. As a disciple, you must spend time daily communing with your Father in order to sustain your energy for the mission of Jesus. My son expects you to devote time to serving others, especially those in need. The gifts you are blessed with are meant to be shared. They are not for your pleasure alone. If you can cook, prepare meals for the homeless and hungry. If you can sing, join the church choir. If you can teach, volunteer to teach religion.

Disciples try to resemble the poor Christ. They do not hoard their money and possessions but are generous in donating them to others. As if that weren't enough, Jesus asks you to surrender your heart and your will to him. He also expects you to follow his law of love, which may result in being mocked and persecuted.

Dear, your happiness lies in being a fervent disciple. Enlist my aid. I pray that love for Jesus will impel you to stay faithful to him no matter what it costs you.

Tell Mary what you find difficult about being a follower of her son.

Perk Up

December 3

My child, sometimes apparently for no reason at all you are sad. The sun may be shining, but an ugly gray cloud is parked over your head. That is normal. You might put on a happy face for others, but I hear your sighs. When you are dejected, you can always find solace in my arms. I love you with all my heart, and your sadness makes me sad. I long to dispel your bad mood. Stay with me awhile. Rest your head on my pure heart and hear it beating with love for you. Let's dwell on pleasant thoughts.

What are some of your happiest memories? Who are the people who love you? Where have you been that brought joy to your heart?

My advice for you is twofold. First, make sure you are caring for your physical well-being—getting enough sleep, eating right, and exercising. Second, perform an act of kindness for someone. That will take your mind off yourself and lift your spirits. When you are happy, you are an enlivening presence for others, a blessing to them. Joy is contagious.

ℭ *Share with Mary your answers to the questions she posed.*

While Waiting

December 4

My child, like all mothers, I had to wait nine months before Jesus made his appearance. Those months before I would see his little face seemed to stretch out like years. I thought about him and wondered at the miracle taking place within me, especially after I felt his first kick.

You must wait for various things, such as a visit, a green light, mail, a phone call, and the result of a test or a job interview. You find it irritating to have to wait for the doctor to see you and for your turn at the checkout counter. As a product of a culture that prizes speed and efficiency, you especially dislike waiting. You think of all the things you could be doing instead.

While you wait, why not spend time pondering Jesus who lives within you? Speak to him as I did while he was growing inside me. Or you might speak to me, dear. Conversing with people who love you will make the time pass more quickly and gracefully.

As the people of old awaited the Messiah, you wait for him too in his second coming. Use your time well!

ଔ *Talk to Mary about what you are waiting for currently.*

Discipline

December 5

My child, being a disciple requires discipline, that is to say, self-control. You need to curb your tendency to take the easier route and force yourself to do what is challenging. Jesus demands what might look impossible. He tells you to take up your cross, to love others whether they love you or not, and when struck to turn the other cheek. He sends you out to preach his message of good news even if you are painfully shy and even if the world around you is a moral wasteland and people will laugh at you and call you foolish.

By repeatedly taking yourself in hand and succeeding in living as my son taught, you will gain facility in performing the good you naturally resist. Consequently, you will reach the wholeness you desire. You will shine like a diamond.

Granted, you will never be perfect, my darling. You will have lapses and flaws, but even your greatest faults can't separate me from you. I will never give up on you. With my help and motherly persistence, you will become a Christian who is an inspiration to others.

ᖇ *Share with Mary what impedes your progress in being a full-hearted disciple.*

Leaving the Mountaintop

December 6

My child, you might have had an experience of God that took your breath away. Perhaps you were at prayer and had an overwhelming sense of his presence and love. Or maybe God answered your prayers in a way far beyond what you expected. The mystical event made you giddy, and the glow might have lasted for some time. But then, all too soon you fell back into the daily routine.

This is what happened to the three apostles when Jesus let them see him transfigured on the mountaintop. They wanted to stay there, but they couldn't. They had to go down the mountain and back to work.[62]

Treasure and cling onto those special moments with God. Thank him for them and let them give you the impetus to strive to love him and please him. The joy you felt then was just a foretaste of the bliss that awaits you in your eternal homeland. My moments with the Angel Gabriel were extraordinary, but then I too had to resume the ordinary life of a Jewish wife and mother. I promise to see you through all your highs and lows. Hopefully you will sense my loving presence.

୨ *Share with Mary a time when you felt very close to God.*

---

[62] Matthew 17:1–9

Examining the Heart

December 7

My child, my sincere wish for you is that you become as holy as you can. Keep up the struggle against forces that pull you away from the dream God has for you. I will be like a shield for you. Aim to grow strong in the virtues that make you more like Jesus and me. This is a lifelong endeavor, and it takes constant vigilance.

One practice I recommend to you, dear, is to examine your heart every evening. Review the highpoints of the day and be honest in admitting where you could have done better. Also review the things you did for which you are proud. As you examine your heart, I will be with you alerting you to faults you may have forgotten or didn't realize. I will also congratulate you on the victories you had.

By paying attention to your daily life, your triumphs and your reversals, you will come to know yourself better. You will be more apt to improve as a person and deepen your spiritual life. Look to me to help you make quick progress. I won't disappoint you.

ℭ *Ask Mary to help you develop the habit of examining your conscience each night.*

The Privilege of Purity
Immaculate Conception
December 8

My child, God wants you to be completely filled with holiness, his divine life. That is your life's goal: to be spiritually pure with no taint of sin marring the beauty of your soul. I was free from sin from the first moment of my existence. Because it was only right that the Son of God become incarnate in a pure vessel, the merits Jesus won were anticipated in me. I could identify myself to St. Bernadette at Lourdes as the Immaculate Conception.

Maybe you are a little skeptical that there was a woman who never sinned. Do you know someone so good, so kind, that you can't imagine him or her doing anything wrong? If so, then a first-century woman like me could be sinless too. What I am, you are called to be, my dear child.

Total sanctity is not beyond your reach. I will pray that such an immense love for God blooms in your heart that you shrink from sin. I will also ask the Holy Spirit within you to ignite the virtues that make you invincible in the battle against sin. With my loving assistance, you too can succeed in having an immaculate heart.

cʒ *Talk to Mary about your desire to be free from sin. Pray: By your holy and immaculate conception, O Mary, deliver us from evil.*

A Home for Jesus
Translation of the Holy House of Loreto

December 9

My child, I kept house for Jesus for about thirty years. I made and washed his clothing, cooked and served him meals, and cleaned our two-room home. Jesus took up residence in your heart on the day you were committed to him in baptism. He lives in the depths of your being, assisting you to live well and to bear the burdens of life gracefully. Jesus abides in you constantly as long as you don't deliberately evict him by serious sin.

Be good to my Jesus and make him feel welcome. He waits patiently for you to pay attention to him. Speak to him frequently. Tell him how much you appreciate him and all he's done for you. Declare your love for him. Keep your soul beautiful by practicing virtues. Imitate my faithfulness, humility, and charity. With all my heart I hope that someday when you approach the gates of heaven, my son will meet you there, extend his arms to you, herald you into his home, saying, "Come in. Come in. You remind me so much of my mother."

ɔʒ *Enlist Mary's aid in being a good host to her son. Ask her to help you cultivate a particular one of her virtues.*

A Just Anger

December 10

My child, periodically you are overcome with anger and see red. A bumbling clerk can't get your order straight. A child misbehaves for the umpteenth time. A car is tailgating you. Any number of irritations can cause you to lose control. Lashing out in anger at other people can be sinful and is bad for your health. When your patience is on the verge of running out, send a swift prayer to me. I will see that you remain calm and unruffled.

Some anger is righteous anger when the occasion calls for it. My son was incensed because selling of livestock and doves, exchanging Gentile money, and probably cheating were going on within the precincts of his Father's holy Temple. You know how he overturned tables and drove out animals.[63]

You are right to be angry at the corruption in your world. Heinous crimes like human trafficking and murder demand that you take action. That is what Jesus would do. When an opportunity arises where you can fight injustice, I will give you a shake and say, "Get moving. There's work to be done." Funnel your anger into positive action.

ের *Talk to Mary about steps you can take to right a wrong, perhaps within your own family.*

---

[63] John 2:14–17

God Alone

December 11

My child, God is the supreme one in your life. Your very existence and your every breath depend on him. Everything you enjoy on earth is a gift from him. God deserves to be on center stage in your heart. It would be foolish to replace him with a human being; a worldly goal like wealth, fame, or success; or yourself.

My life naturally revolved around the Son of God. My whole being was dedicated to loving and serving him, his Father, and his Spirit. Your whole being should too. When you are tempted to idolize someone or something other than God and erect a temple to this false god in your heart, I will join forces with you to combat that urge. I will redirect your gaze to the only One who is all good, all pure, and all beautiful. I will remind you that God loves you with a tremendous love and delights in you. He is a jealous lover who desires your whole, undivided heart.

Confirm your love for God every day by offering him yourself and all you do. Foster your love for him by frequent contact. Make a solid relationship with him your sole overriding ambition.

Tell Mary of your desire to adore God alone. Ask her help in keeping him number one in your life.

Mother to All
Our Lady of Guadalupe

December 12

My child, I came to the peasant St. Juan Diego on Tepeyac Hill in Mexico as a brown-skinned Aztec woman garbed in Indian clothing including a black sash, the sign of pregnancy. I wanted to underscore that I am mother to all peoples, no matter what race or nationality. I asked to have a church built on the hill there where I could see people's tears and enable them to know a mother's heart and be consoled and at peace.

When Juan Diego was worried about his dying uncle, I healed him. When Juan asked for a sign, I provided roses in winter. Juan's tilma that bears my miraculously preserved image is displayed in Mexico City.

You, my darling, are one of my beloved children. Never hesitate to come to me with your problems, worries, disappointments, and sorrows. Although I will not appear to you in a visible form, I assure you I am alive and real. I may see to it that you experience miracles as St. Juan Diego did. I love you no less than I love him and will gladly unburden you. Your concerns are my concerns. And I would like it very much if you made my concern for people of every country your concern.

ca *Talk to Mary about anything weighing on your heart.*

Blue for Peace

December 13

My child, blue is the most popular color. God must favor it too. He used it lavishly in creation, coloring both the wide expanses of sky and oceans blue. Blue is associated with me although Nazareth clothing made of natural fibers was cream-colored. Blue dye was expensive.

When Byzantine empresses wore blue, artists gave me blue clothing to reflect that I am Queen of Heaven and Earth. The Ark of the Covenant where God resided was covered with blue cloth. When Jesus dwelt within me, I was a flesh-and-blood ark, so blue is fitting for me. In apparitions at Fatima and Mexico, I wore a blue mantle.

Blue, a comforting color, stands for calm and peace. When you are in a tizzy—bedeviled by problems or overwhelmed by work, gaze at the blue sky or sit by a blue body of water or in a blue room. Little by little peace will soak into you. Better still, think of me, the Queen of Peace. Know you are in good and loving hands, your mother's hands. My prayers for your serenity and my tender hugs will bring peace to your troubled heart. Your worries and fears will disappear like burst soap bubbles. You will stride calmly into the future, whatever it may hold.

CR *Talk to Mary about where you and the world need peace.*

Expecting God

December 14

My child, you celebrate the coming of Jesus at Christmas and look forward to his coming again at the end of time. But don't forget, Jesus comes to you in mystery in many forms, most prominently in the Eucharist. Jesus also comes to you personally in other people. The harried clerk in the store, the neighbor asking you to feed her dogs while she's away, or the sister who is laid up with a broken leg—all are my son asking for help. When you show love for any person, he considers it done for him.

You never know when or how Jesus will appear. He might be disguised as a dirty man in ragged clothes or a woman from another country who has an accent. Be ready to respond with your whole heart. Pesky reasons for not helping someone in need may weasel their way into your mind, such as I don't have time or another person would do a better job. Think of me traveling to help Elizabeth while I was pregnant. In your situation ask, "What would Mary do?" I hope that I will inspire you to ignore any excuses and welcome Jesus with open arms and a smile on your face.

ℭ? *Talk to Mary about recognizing Jesus in people you know.*

Gloomy Days

December 15

My dear, maybe you are crushed by the weight of the world's problems—the evil pervading it, the threat of war, and the devastation of the environment. Perhaps your own hardships are unrelenting and you have scant hope for improvement. It could be your self-worth has dwindled because of your repeated faults, mistakes, and failures. Any of these possibilities can lead to full-blown depression. Whenever discouragement overtakes you, don't succumb, darling. I will stretch out my loving hand to catch you. Grab hold of it before you tumble into a dark, damp pit.

Your heavenly Father has a special blueprint for your life. As you live it out, you will be challenged to endure crosses. These can potentially lead you to deeper levels of faith. With God's grace which I will implore for you, all will work out well. Be patient and persist although you feel as though you are lost in a thick blanket of fog. From my vantage point, I see hope on the horizon for you. Eventually Jesus, the light of the world, will dispel your gloom. Trust me. My son has your welfare at heart, and so do I.

 os *Share with Mary anything causing you distress.*

Excusing Others

December 16

My child, people get under your skin by saying or doing something you frown upon. Before even a trace of resentment appears in your heart, I urge you to excuse them. See the spark of God in them and make an excuse for their behavior. After all, aren't you are quick to make exceptions for yourself?

You are probably thinking that ignoring others' faults is a daunting task. I will help you grit your teeth and overlook the minor infractions. Many a time I had to do this. A customer at a crowded market stall would push against me, and instead of giving her a nasty look or giving her a shove back, I thought, Well, maybe she lost her balance! The next time you see someone speed through a red light, you might imagine that they are on the way to the hospital.

Keep in mind, my darling, that the faults in others that annoy you most could be the very faults you have. I love all my children and accept the fact that you are not perfect. I think that sometimes you are harder on yourself than God is. So don't worry about others or yourself!

❧ *Talk to Mary about others' actions that are your pet peeves.*

The Extra Mile

December 17

My child, love goes beyond what is required or expected and sometimes beyond what is reasonable. Look at the lengths God went to because of his love for us. Jesus asks his followers to go overboard too when it comes to showing love. He taught, "If anyone forces you to go one mile, go also the second mile."[64] This reminds me of the time Jesus joined the two disciples traveling to Emmaus. They accepted this stranger's company, but then they also invited him to stay with them overnight and dine with them. The two were not obliged to be this kind, and supposedly they would derive no benefit from it.

When the Holy Spirit inspires you to go the extra mile, I pray that you cooperate. This means that when someone asks a favor, you not only oblige but surprise them with an added gift. If you are invited to work a shift feeding the hungry at a shelter, you cover two shifts. If you receive a call asking for a twenty-five dollar donation, you give fifty. The reward for your generosity awaits you in heaven. On earth often you will have nothing more than a warm, satisfied feeling and a loving embrace from me.

ෆ *Explore with Mary when you might go the extra mile.*

---

[64] Matthew 5:41

365

Hurt Feelings

December 18

My child, inevitably people will hurt your feelings. They will criticize something you did or something about you. If your critic is a person you admire, the arrow stings more sharply. If you are sensitive, you may be thrown into a tailspin and fall into a deep well of sorrow. The hurtful words play over and over in your mind. You think of what you could have said to defend yourself, or worse, you decide to cut ties with the one who hurt you. You might shed tears.

Sweetheart, I ache for you when you experience this. I long to clasp you to my heart and gently remove the arrow. I understand your pain. When I was pregnant, people looked askance at me. Later, people said horrid things about my son, and that hurt me to the quick.

As time passes, your wound will heal. In the meantime, analyze what happened and see if there isn't a grain of truth in the negative comment. Put your uncomfortable feelings to good use by offering them for an intention such as world peace. You might even pray for the person who offended you. That is what a true child of mine would do, dear.

ఴ *Review with Mary memories you have of hurtful comments. Ask her to obtain for you the grace of forgiveness.*

Enticements

December 19

My child, I feel sorry for you in that all day long commercials and ads pressure you to purchase goods and services. It is tempting to succumb to their glittery enticements that promise you joy. Still, people who have everything often are restless and unhappy. Jesus warned against possessing the whole world and losing your soul.[65] I would hate to see you becoming less than you were meant to be and endangering your eternal life.

Ask for my assistance in resisting temptations to have the latest and the best. With my help, you can curb your desire to accumulate more and more to the point that you don't even know what is in your closets or storage pods. You will be able to control your tendency to purchase something just because someone else has it.

Hoarding things and buying things you don't need wastes time that could be put to better use. By living simply and sharing what you own with others, especially those in need, you will attain the everlasting joy my son promised. That, darling, is my dream for you.

ભ *Talk to Mary about how you can divest yourself of unnecessary belongings.*

---

[65] Matthew 16:26

Kingdom Builder

December 20

My child, in my lifetime, Jesus inaugurated the kingdom of God on earth. It is the reign of God in which justice, peace, and love prevail. You, dear, are a citizen of this kingdom and my son's ambassador in advancing it. You are fully aware that things are not what they should be. I beg you to take the initiative in establishing God's kingdom. Yes, the challenge is enormous, and you might feel helpless. But we depend on you to make a difference.

The building blocks for this ideal kingdom are easily accessible. The Holy Spirit provides them. They are the virtues faith, hope, charity, justice, fortitude, prudence, and temperance. When you practice any of these, you further the kingdom.

When you tire of working for a better world or when you are discouraged at the lack of results, come to me. Release your difficulties into my hands. I will refresh you so that you rise with a renewed resolve to pierce the darkness around you with the light of Christ's justice and peace. Even changing just one issue or one person's heart for the better is valuable. My son and I love you for it.

ભ *Talk over with Mary ways you can advance God's kingdom.*

Christ in You

December 21

My child, I gave birth to Jesus in Bethlehem, but you are to bring him to birth in your own time. You do this by letting people see Christ in you. You conform yourself to him.

My son had a tender heart for the poor and marginalized. When you reach out to care for all those in need and love even the most repulsive, people see Christ. Jesus was not afraid to stand up for what was right even when it meant flouting the standards of his culture. When you fight for justice at the risk of being accused and scorned, people see Christ. Jesus taught about our heavenly Father and his kingdom. When you spread the good news, people see Christ. Jesus was a person of prayer. When you make time to go to church and to pray in public and in private, people see Christ.

As I guided the growth of Jesus, I will foster his life in you. I, your devoted heavenly mother, will watch over you and pray that the qualities that distinguished my son shine forth in your life with a brilliance that attracts others to him.

cx *What quality in Christ do you especially wish to emulate? Speak to Mary about it.*

Fork in the Road

December 22

My child, as you travel the journey of your life, sometimes you come to a fork in the road. You must decide which way to go. When one direction is a good, life-giving option and the other is a bad, death-dealing option, you know which one I fervently hope you take. I will do my utmost to steer you in that direction. I will pray that fear, pride, or lust do not cloud your reasoning. Even if you make the wrong choice, I will not abandon you but continue to love you and coax you to reverse directions until you are safe again.

Sometimes, a fork offers you a choice between two or more morally neutral paths. You might need to decide on a college, a career, a house, or a spouse. In cases like these, as you weigh the pros and cons and consult others, remember to take me into consideration. Ask me to pray that you make the choice that will yield the most good fruit in your life, the choice that will lead to a more dynamic relationship with God and more happiness. I always want what is best for you, my darling.

cx *Talk to Mary about a decision facing you presently or in the near future.*

Dealing with Surprises
December 23

My child, who would ever think that when I was nine months pregnant, Joseph and I would need to make a weeklong journey? The emperor ordered people to go to their ancestors' land for a census. Because Joseph was from King David's family, he had to stop work and travel to Bethlehem. How frustrated he was! Not wanting to be apart from Joseph at this critical time, I went with him. I could have given birth at the side of the road.

You probably know by now to expect the unexpected. When an odd turn of events crops up, muster all the courage you can and deal with it. Just as I accompanied Joseph, I will be with you on your life's journey. At times your path may be rough, uphill, and full of detours, but never fear. I will be your guide on your way to paradise, your first parents' original home.

At the end of our trip to Bethlehem, I saw the face of Jesus for the first time. At the end of your earthly journey, you will see him face-to-face. All of your trials will have been worth this vision.

ɑ℈ *Talk to Mary about an unforeseen problem that confronted you or one that you are coping with now.*

Love Made Flesh

December 24

My child, some things are so awesome that words fail us. Imagine what it was like to hold my newborn son in my arms knowing he was the Son of God. Joseph and I were silent before this tremendous miracle. How great is the love that compelled God to become one of us, his mortal creatures.

Mentally kneel at the wooden manger and gaze down on the infant Jesus sound asleep on some hay. Marvel at his little nose, his delicate eyelashes, his tiny fingernails. Watch his chest rise and fall with each breath. Know that within that chest is a heart of flesh beating with love for you.

Let your heart overflow with love for God and thankfulness. In your mind remain there in silent adoration. I will be there too, looking at both you and Jesus with quiet joy. I am elated that I was privileged to play such a huge role in your salvation. Be still and savor resting in your vision of the Bethlehem nursery. In the silence of that night, stay rapt in adoration as long as you can. When you can linger no longer, carry away with you the peace of that scene. Let it spill over from your heart into your home.

⅓ *Speak to Mary about the magic and mystery of her first*
  night with her son.

Spreading Joy
Christmas

December 25

My child, when Jesus restored the possibility of eternal life to the human race, all creation rejoiced. My heart, too, was filled with gladness. You celebrate the Christmas season with friends and family in honor of the saving event. It is a time to bring cheer to everyone but especially to those who are not as fortunate as you. I would like you to forget about your own happiness and concentrate on giving joy to others, not just at Christmas but every day.

With that attitude, you do not care about amassing treasures for yourself. You are not bothered if you give someone a gift or do a favor and it is not returned. Rather, you go out of your way to spread joy. Invite a lonely person to share a meal with you. Perform a random act of kindness. Compliment someone. Renew your relationship with a person who dropped out of your family or circle of friends. Present someone with an unexpected gift.

By bringing joy to others, a sweet joy will bubble up in your own heart. You will also make me very happy, my dear.

ɑ჻ *Talk to Mary about how people have made you happy and ways you can spread joy.*

Caring for Creatures

December 26

My child, tabby cats have an *M* on their forehead. A charming legend is that on Christmas night a tabby cat crept into the manger. There he kept baby Jesus warm and purred him to sleep. I showed my gratitude by marking the cat with my initial.

It's interesting that the first to behold the Savior of the world besides Joseph and me were the animals whose cave we shared. God made all the fantastic creatures on earth from the tiniest bug to the largest dinosaur. He saved them from the flood in Noah's time, and Jesus redeemed them along with all creation.

Animals belong to God, but he entrusted them into our care. This includes any pet of yours. I appreciated the lamb that provided wool, the goat that gave us milk and cheese, and the donkey that carried us on our journeys. Jesus, Joseph, and I took good care of them.

Today many animals are mistreated and endangered, which saddens me and angers God. You might donate to a fund that works to defend them or adopt a rescue dog. I will help you to be a good steward of God's world. Someday he will thank you.

ᘓ *Talk to Mary about the animals in your life and ways you can protect your fellow creatures.*

Life Is Precious

December 27

My child, I remember well that night in Bethlehem when I first saw my son. I had wondered if he would look and act unusual because he was God's Son too. But no. Jesus was like an ordinary baby—red, wrinkled, crying, and hungry. Still, he was a miracle made from my flesh and blood and God's power with no man's assistance.

When you think of it, every newborn is a miracle: a unique creation in whom the characteristics of a man and a woman are combined. What an ingenious way God devised to multiply the human race! The practice of snuffing out new life while it is still developing in the womb is abhorrent to me. All human beings are precious, from their beginning stages to their final hours. And all human beings belong to God our Father who created them. How can anyone dare to usurp his authority?

You enjoy the gift of life. Do what you can to afford other people the same privilege. I will join forces with you to promote respect for life. Together we can change a culture of death in small increments.

ଔ *Talk to Mary about what it means to be pro-life and what you can do to protect life.*

Prayer for Good Governments
Feast of the Holy Innocents
December 28

My child, King Herod was an unscrupulous, heartless ruler, who massacred babies to protect his throne. Only through God's intervention did Joseph and I save Jesus by escaping to Egypt. My heart bleeds for those parents who never saw their children grow up. Rulers of some countries today are guilty of the deaths of thousands, including innocent men, women, and children. I weep for these victims too, who are all my children.

I know that you are horrified by the flagrant evil in the world but feel quite helpless. You aren't helpless. I, the mother of Christ the King, am a powerful lifeline to him. So pray to me—especially the Rosary, consecrate yourself to me, and offer acts of penance for the intention of world peace. Also, take whatever other steps you can to change corrupt or unjust governments and to protect the innocent.

In every Our Father prayer, you pray, "Thy kingdom come." As a member of God's family, you are responsible for promoting his kingdom of peace and justice on earth. This is your Father's dream for the world and also mine. Together we can make it happen.

ଔ *What actions can you take to further God's kingdom on earth? Talk with Mary about them.*

Procrastination

December 29

My child, procrastinating is a common human fault. Maybe you tend to put off high priority tasks and fill your time with trivial ones. You may decide to wait until you are in the right mood to tackle a major item on your to do list. You trick yourself in thinking you will take care of the important job later, but later might turn into never.

I want to help you combat procrastination, sweetheart, because it hinders you from being all that you could be. For example, the Holy Spirit may inspire you to join an organization that assists the needy. Then you distract yourself by engaging in other activities. Or you defer your prayer time in order to do household chores. What I am most concerned about are the times you intend to break a bad habit, but day after day you promise yourself you will start tomorrow.

I will give you a little push to get you moving toward your goal, and I will hold your hand along the way. Imagine how relieved you will be when the task is behind you. Besides, you will feel better about yourself.

CR *What necessary job are you delaying? Ask Mary to help you accomplish it soon.*

Cherish Your Family
The Holy Family

December 30
Or the Sunday between Christmas and January 1

My child, with the Son of God as a family member, you can imagine how peaceful our Nazareth home was. There were no arguments, mean little digs, foul moods, or accusations. Jesus, Joseph, and I tried to outdo one another in showing love. While the two men supported me as construction workers, I kept them fed and clothed. My delight was in making them happy.

Your family, too, has been personally chosen by God, and your chief responsibility is to help one another become saints. Declare your love for your family often and express it in deeds. Support, encourage, and comfort the members when it is needed. Pray for your family and plan times when you pray together. Spend time with your family members, especially at meals. Never let different opinions or mistakes sever the ties between you and a family member. Be quick to ask for forgiveness and to extend it. Stay in touch, and if a member is estranged, be the first to reach out.

Depend on me to send graces your way that will facilitate making your family a holy family too. Then you will impact the world as we did.

ভ *Talk to Mary about your family relationships, in particular what you can do to strengthen them.*

The Gift of Time

December 31

My child, time is just a tiny piece of eternity. In it you are allotted a certain number of years to live. You don't know exactly when your stay on earth to perfect yourself will be over. My aim is to help you grow holier as you grow older.

Let's ponder the last twelve months together. You've had some wonderful experiences when you danced along merrily. But sometimes you were mired in adversities and you trudged through the hours. You accomplished some wonderful things, but also made some mistakes.

The next twelve months lie before you like empty pages waiting for you to write the story of your life. Forge into this new year with high hopes and an intention to improve at least one aspect of your life. One resolution I hope you make is to remain close to me. I cherish the time you spend with me, sharing your life. With all my heart, I look forward to the day you cross the threshold of the next world and I can tell you of my love face-to-face.

ଔ *Talk to Mary about your prospects and plans for the next twelve months.*

Walking with Mary
A Group Retreat

Adapt the following plan to your group. Choose activities according to the length of the retreat, which could run for a morning, an afternoon, an evening, one day, or a weekend. Provide refreshments or a meal.

Make blue (Mary's color) the predominant color: blue tablecloths, napkins, folders, candles, and vigil lights.

Room Set Up

- Round tables to facilitate discussion during faith sharing
- Centerpiece on each table with any of these items: a vigil light, a scarf, a Marian image or prayer card, a plant
- Prayer table with an image of Mary, a Bible, a candle, flowers, and a basket or box
- CDs with Marian songs
- Marian slides (optional)
- Equipment for music and a slide show (optional)
- Microphone if the group is large
- Lectern

The Program

- Cover: Retreat title, time and place, picture of Mary
- Back: The schedule with break times noted
- Inside: Questions for faith sharing
            Prayers to Mary
            Marian poems
            Quotations about Mary
            Resources: Bibliography of books about Mary
                        Marian websites
                        Marian shrines nearby

Participant Supplies

- Name badges that bear Mary's image or symbol, felt-tipped pens, wastebasket
- Folder labeled with the title of the retreat and a picture of Mary and containing writing paper, prayers, pen, and an evaluation form
- Paper heart for each person, placed on tables or chairs
- Materials for beaded or corded rosaries (optional)
- Copy of the book *Heart to Heart with Mary* (optional)
- Hymnals or song sheet
- Mementoes of the retreat, such as Marian medals, holy cards, rosary rings, Marian flowers or their seeds

The Schedule

I. Introduction

Welcome everyone to this time spent honoring Mary, Mother of God, and getting to know her better.

Introduce the leader(s).

Ask the retreatants to introduce themselves by stating their name and one fact about themselves.

Tell the location of the chapel and restrooms.

II. Opening Prayer

Begin with the Sign of the Cross.

Holy Spirit, through your power
the Blessed Virgin Mary conceived Jesus
and God became a human being to save us.
Be with us today as we ponder this woman
chosen to bring forth the Word into the world.
Open our hearts to listen to your personal
message for us
and give us the courage to act on it.
In this way we will imitate Mary
and bring forth Jesus in our corner of the world.
Help us to deepen our love and appreciation
for God's Mother, who is also our mother. Amen.

III. Intentions

Explain:

You could be home now gardening, watching a video, or taking a nap. Instead you chose to nourish your spiritual life by attending this retreat on Mary. Retreats are pleasing to God, grace-filled, and powerful. You are invited to offer this time for an intention. This could be a living or deceased loved one in need of prayers, a special intention for yourself, or world peace.

Mary is our intercessor and our prayers go through her hands to God. Write your intention or a key word for it on the paper heart. Then fold the heart and walk up to the prayer table and place the heart in the basket by Mary's image.

(Play a Marian song as the retreatants process to the prayer table.)

After everyone is seated, pray the Hail Mary.

IV. Main Activities

1. Read a page from *Heart to Heart with Mary*. Invite the retreatants to write a response to Mary or to quietly meditate on the passage. Repeat as often as time allows.

2. Have the retreatants discuss questions at the tables.

Questions for Faith Sharing

1. How has your concept of Mary changed over the years? How has your relationship with her changed?
2. Has Mary ever answered your prayers? How?
3. What is your favorite Marian prayer? What is your favorite title of hers?
4. When have you said yes to God and trusted like Mary did? What happened?
5. What aspect of Mary's life speaks most to you?
6. Have you visited a Marian shrine, such as Lourdes or Fatima? If so, what impressed you?
7. Who reminds you of Mary? In what way?

V. Conclusion

Pray a prayer to Mary such as the Angelus, the Magnificat, or the Memorare and sing a Marian hymn such as "Immaculate Mary."

Distribute mementoes of the retreat.

Collect evaluation forms.

Ten Supplementary Activities

1. Arrange for an individual or a panel to speak about what our Blessed Mother means to them.

2. Make books and pamphlets about Our Lady available for retreatants to read during quiet times.

3. Show slides related to Mary: pictures of the Holy Land, images of Mary under her various titles, statues from the shrines of the Basilica of the Immaculate Conception in Washington, D.C.

4. Make rosaries while listening to Marian songs.

5. Pray the Rosary, maybe as a Living Rosary.

6. Pray a Marian Way of the Cross.

7. Show a video about Mary, perhaps the story of one of her apparitions.

8. Carry out a May Crowning.

9. Read aloud poems about Mary from the program or handouts. Suggestions: "Litany for the Ordinary" by Irene Zimmerman and "Before Jesus Was His Mother" from *Living God's Justice* by Alla Renée Bozarth.

10. Ask the participants to write their names on slips of paper, stones, or shells, deposit them in a box, and then as the box is passed around, draw out a name for a person to pray for during the coming year.

Notes